NEW FORMATIONS

EDITOR:
David Glover

GUEST EDITORS:
Phil Cohen & Bill Schwarz

EDITORIAL ASSISTANT
Alyson Pendlebury

EDITORIAL BOARD:
Lesley Caldwell
Laura Chrisman
Jeremy Gilbert
Cora Kaplan
Scott McCracken
Ali Rattansi
Bill Schwarz
Judith Squires
Jenny Bourne Taylor
Wendy Wheeler

ADVISORY BOARD:
Ien Ang
Angelika Bammer
Tony Bennett
Jody Berland
Homi Bhabha
Victor Burgin
Hazel Carby
Erica Carter
Iain Chambers
John Copjec
Lidia Curti
Tony Davies
James Donald
Simon Frith
Stuart Hall
Dick Hebdige
Edward Said
Renata Saleci
Gayatri Chakravorty Spivak
Valerie Walkerdine

New Formations is
published three times
a year by
Lawrence & Wishart
99a Wallis Road
London E9 5LN
Tel: 0181-533 2506
Fax: 0181-533 7369

GW00360073

ADVERTISEMENTS:
For enquiries/bookings contact Sally Davis
Lawrence & Wishart

SUBSCRIPTION:
For 1998, subscription rates to Lawrence &
are, for 3 issues
UK: Institutions £70, Individuals £35.
Rest of world: Institutions £75; Individuals £38.
Single copies: £14.99

CONTRIBUTIONS AND CORRESPONDENCE:
Send to:
The Editor, *New Formations*
Dept. of English, University of Southampton
Highfield, Southampton SO17 1BJ

BOOKS FOR REVIEW:
Send to:
Alasdair Pettinger
Scottish Music Information Centre
1 Bowmont Gardens
Glasgow, Scotland G12 9LR

Prospective writers are encouraged to contact the
editors to discuss their ideas and to obtain a copy of
our style sheet.
Manuscripts should be sent in triplicate. They will
not be returned unless a stamped, self-addressed
envelope is enclosed. Contributors should note that
the editorial board cannot take responsibility for any
manuscript submitted to *New Formations*.

ISSN   0 950 2376
ISBN   0 5315 8584

Text design and setting by Derek Doyle & Associates,
Mold, Flintshire.
Printed in Great Britain at the University Press,
Cambridge.

NOTES ON CONTRIBUTORS

Lorraine Ayensu was born in Manchester of Ghanaian and English parentage and was brought up by a voluntary child-care agency in the north-east of England. She is a social worker, freelance consultant, singer and song-writer.

Les Back teaches in the Department of Sociology at Goldsmiths College. He is the author of *New Ethnicities* and *Urban Youth Culture*.

David A Bailey is a cultural critic, curator and artist. He currently works with the black archive at the University of East London and has just curated a major exhibition at the Hayward Gallery on the Harlem Renaissance.

Mary Chamberlain is Professor of History at Oxford Brookes University. She is the author of *Narratives of Exile and Return*.

Phil Cohen is Reader in Cultural Studies at the University of East London, where he heads the Centre for New Ethnicities Research. He co-edited *Multi-Racist Britain* and his latest book is *Rethinking the Youth Question*.

Sunil Gupta is a Canadian citizen who was born in India and lives and works as an artist, curator and editor in London. The last book he edited was *Disrupted Borders*. He works as a curator for the Organization for Visual Arts.

Stuart Hall has recently retired as Professor of Sociology at the Open University.

Barnor Hesse is Senior Lecturer in Sociology at the University of East London and is the co-author of *Beneath the Surface: racial harassment*.

Jayne O. Ifekwunigwe was born in London of Nigerian and Irish-English-Guyanese parentage. She is a lecturer in sociology and anthropology at the University of East London. She is self-taught in visual-art installation and in photographic collage.

Tunde Jegede was born in London of Yoruba and English parentage. He is now a musician, having studied the cello and the kora since the age of seven. He is both a composer and recording artist – *Lamentation* and *Malian Royal Court Music* have appeared on Triciom Records.

Kenan Malik is a freelance journalist who writes regularly for the *Guardian* and the *New Statesman*. He is the author of *The Meaning of Race*.

Sue Rosner is the Head of Drama at Plashet School.

Bill Schwarz teaches at Goldsmiths College.

Folake Shoga was born in Ibadan, Nigeria of Yoruba and English parents, and is now a visual artist, film-maker and animator.

Shanti Thomas was born in London of Indian and Italian parents, studied art in Italy and England and is now an artist. Her paintings are associated with emotions and bodily experiences and with the cycles of growth and decay, life and death. She is now studying for an MA in European Art in Barcelona and Winchester.

Gucharan Virdee teaches anthropology at the University of East London and researches on women and Hindi cinema.

Nira Yuval-Davis is Professor of Gender and Ethnic Studies at the University of Greenwich. She is the co-author of *Racialised Boundaries* and the author of *Gender and Nation*.

CONTENTS
NUMBER 33 SPRING 1998

ACKNOWLEDGEMENTS

We would like to thank Michael Rustin, Dean of the Faculty of Social Science at the University of East London, for his encouragement and support in organising the conference. We would also like to thank Jagdish Gundara from The International Centre for Intercultural Studies at the Institute of Education for his work in facilitating the conference and for his personal contribution. The Youth Arts programme was supported by grants from the London Arts Board and the Paul Hamlyn Trust.

Conference Organising Committee: Phil Cohen, Jagdish Gundara, Jayne Ifekwunigwe, Linda Rosmovitz, Ashwani Sharma, Gucharan Virdee.

Plenary and Workshop Contributors: Patience Agbabi, Lorraine Ayensu, Malika B, David A Bailey, Jatinder Barn, Les Back, Alice Bloch, Marc Boothe, Mary Boushel, Mary Chamberlain, Phil Cohen, Jonzi D, Costas Douzinas, Peter Fitzpatrick, Paul Gilroy, Jagdish Gundara, Sunil Gupta, Catherine Hall, Stuart Hall, Barnor Hesse, Roger Hewitt, Mary Hickman, Eva Hoffman, Jayne Ifekwunigwe, Lee Jasper, Tunde Jegede, Kanta Kaur, Michael Keith, Funmilayo Kolaro, Kenan Malik, Paul McPherson, Phil Marfleet, John Marriott, Simon and Ngozi Onwurah, Ingrid Pollard, Linda Rozmovits, Folake Shoga, Bill Schwarz, Iain Sinclair, Shanti Thomas, Patricia Tuitt, Gucharan Virdee, Lola Young, Nira Yuval-Davis, Siobhan Wall.

Media Inputs: Dave Mann, Andy Minnion, Olamide Pratt, Weinau Tesfu, Anne Vinje, Anna Von Eichenwald, Kin-Man Ly, Yvonne Connike, Andrew Ward, Pat Desmond, Ruth Lawes.

Conference Administration: Tim Lucas, Tahmina Maula, Sarah Newlands, Linda John, Alice Henshaw.

Youth Arts Programme: Geoff Brunell, Andrew Mutter, Lilly Elianne, Gordon Edwards, Jonathon Archibald, Davina Purin, Sandra Shevlin, Mary Jo Ovington, Angela Thompson, Maureen Otwell, Alison Vickers, Margaret Armstrong, Petch Phillips, Rayna Nadeem, Chris Christodoulou, Sue Rosner, Alison Henderson, Peter Dick, Jane Lee, Linda Brunell, Ashia Oozeer.

EDITORIAL

In December 1996 the Centre for New Ethnicities Research, at the University of East London, organised a conference in collaboration with the International Centre for Inter-Cultural Studies at the Institute of Education in London. Leading scholars, cultural practitioners and community activists from around Britain came together to take ideas about race, nation and ethnicity for a walk across the shifting terrains of 'Frontlines/Backyards'.

The aim was to create the framework for a different, more thoughtful and sensitive kind of public conversation than that which prevails at most academic colloquia or political rallies. Those of us who have spent eighteen years under Conservative rule, attending conferences which either ignored the prevailing political realities in the name of some superior insight on the world, or used these realities as the basis for mutual recrimination, felt that the time had come for a conference with a difference. Frontlines/Backyards would not be a conference dominated by the reading of academic papers, or the rehearsal of prepared political positions. PC posturing and moral admonition would no longer 'rule OK'. We wanted to create a sense of improvisation and excitement about engaging with those issues of politics and culture that had come in from the margins, and which are beginning to redefine what it means to live in this disunited kingdom, as it faces its uncertain future.

For this purpose we designed an event which wove together statements in music, song, poetry, drama, film and dance, together with political analysis, personal testimony and group discussion. Debate was organised around six workshop themes: rewriting histories of the nation; questioning race and generation; the centring of multiple heritages; the exploration of science fiction and dystopias; the significance of geographies of risk, fear and the city; and the consideration of the politics of immigration in the light of the increasing prominence in the late twentieth century of refugees and asylum-seekers.

Overall the event provided a platform for an emergent dialogue between some of the post-1968 generation who have been rethinking these issues in the 1980s, and a younger post-Thatcher generation – most of the 400-strong audience were under thirty – who not only crossed over many of the customary racial and ideological divides, but who moved easily between the worlds of political campaigning, cultural enterprise and academic scholarship in a way that would have been unthinkable a few years ago.

This debate of the generations was given fresh impetus by the Youth Arts Programme. Over two hundred fourteen-to-seventeen year-olds from six schools and youth projects in the East End of London worked with artists-in-residence throughout the autumn to produce an impressive range of paintings, posters, computer-art, and performance pieces based on the conference themes. Their work, and in some cases their presence, added a welcome vitality to the proceedings.

Nevertheless old habits die hard. There were those who wanted the conference to address racism, racism, racism and if every session did not do that, then (some concluded) there must have been some kind of insidious evasion going on. There were others, at the other end of the spectrum, who thought we should just forget about racism altogether and concentrate on celebrating the new ethnicities released by the postmodern turn. There were some who wanted everyone to go back to basic Marxism and reinvent the great wheel of universalism, while others again wished for nothing more than to put Marxism in the dustbin of history or, at best, flirt with its fragments.

Yet even the occasional bout of bad temper and backbiting failed to dampen the generally genial atmosphere. As one participant put it: 'Frontlines/Backyards was an event waiting to happen – it was a cross between a festival and a conference; it released a lot of creative and intellectual energy which is normally dammed up when we fight our own corners'.

Even so, the content of the conference generated its own predictable difficulties. Many of these centred on what could be implied by the conference title itself. Just how were the languages of frontlines and backyards to find common points of reference? How was it possible to move beyond the divisions of hope they represented? How could the discourses of equality and difference be reconciled? Just where did the priorities of academics, artists and activists connect? Was post-colonial textual theory ever going to have anything much to say to refugees and asylum-seekers struggling to survive in multiracist Britain?

In what follows we have tried to convey something of the style and the substance of the engagement with these issues. We have set out to represent the diverse registers in which this two-day conversation was conducted, and to give the reader – abstracted as ever in the mind of journal-editors – some indication of the range of arguments pursued. Inevitably we have had to be selective. Some material – the performance poetry most strikingly – does not translate well into a written-text on the page. And, to give another example, reading Tunde Jegede's text here is no substitute for listening to him play the kora. Those who want to heed Rilke's advice to learn the dance of the mind where 'words melt into what they cannot capture' will have to buy the video that accompanies this issue in order to get the full sense of the creativity of the contributions.

In choosing material for this issue we have concentrated on work which addresses one or more of the core conference themes in an idiom which is consistent with publication in *new formations*, whilst still remaining true to the provenance of the journal. Out of all the possible contributions (over one hundred people were involved in some kind of way) we offer a sample, a rich enough cut'n'mix, we hope, to provide some substantial but still digestible food for further thought.

Who needs an Island?

Phil Cohen

BETWEEN MAP AND TERRITORY

In the confused lexicon of political conflict in the West, one term stands out as constituting a privileged topos, if not a defining trope, of the world we have all but lost.

The Frontline is where barricades are custom-built, and wars of fixed positions waged, where revolutionary vanguards make their first and last stands and where the militarisation of the body politic rules OK. Frontlines tell tales of impasse and breakthrough, attack and defence, progress and retreat. They are where generations of boys have gone to become men, and groups with 'attitude' shake invisible fists 'in your face'. They are where anti-fascist struggles have demonstrated that the forces of reaction 'shall not pass'. Frontline states have battled successfully with settler colonialism in Africa and popular movements in Latin America have fought against their countries becoming backyards of American imperialism. Frontlines continue to be staked out in the heartlands of the western metropolis when and wherever racial confrontations take place.

We are familiar with the imagery and the reality of these struggles, and we are at home with the clear lines that can apparently be drawn here between oppressor and oppressed, baddies and goodies, bourgeoisie and proletariat, white and black, men and women, heterosexual and gay. At the same time we are becoming conversant, if not comfortable, with the notion that it is here finally that the onward march of the labour movement was halted, well short of its more generous goals; drawing the frontline under its own feet labourism became encamped in exclusionary territories of race, nation and ethnicity, creating its own version of the stakeholder society based on indigenous prides of place, or prior claims over local amenity and resource.

Since the 1950s the hegemony of the frontline over the strategic thinking and practical conduct of leftist politics in the West has withered away along with the triumphalist narratives of class struggle that inspired them. May 1968 marked both the end of the frontline as a comprehensive metaphor of struggle, and the emergence of a quite different map of hope, pointing to whole new territories of contestation. As students in the cities of Old Europe tore up the ancient paving stones to create makeshift barricades and defend themselves against the entirely modern violence of the state, they discovered buried underneath their own actions and rhetorics an altogether different geography and history, that of the backyard and the beach.[1]

1. See Alberto Melucci, *Nomads of the Present*, Radius, London 1989; and Phil Cohen, *Rethinking the Youth Question*, Macmillan, London 1997.

Backyards privilege everything that is marginalised by the rhetoric of frontlines. Backyards are where grand narratives of race, nation and empire come down to earth, are relayed or contested in small talk, in nationalisms of the neighbourhood or racist rumour-mongering; here gossip gathers strength, and moral panics put down roots, cultural guerilla wars are waged, and all kinds of personal negotiation and resistance flourish; across the backyard fence even public enemies can sometimes be private friends.

Backyards are also where women have sometimes been allowed to rule, while the men are away 'at the front'; meanwhile on the edges of the familiar matrilocal world, down back alleys, in secret as yet unmade gardens, children come out to play and youth cultures conduct their strange encounters with the Other Kind. Elsewhere, on the beach, pleasures of sun, sea and sex are merged to create a brilliant polymorphous bodyscape, one that is increasingly extended into all the nightspots of the western world (not only discos, clubs and cinemas, but public parks, cruising grounds, and toilets) where ambiguous or transgressive models of sexuality are the new lords of the dance. Yet even and especially here, where desire is sovereign, the more intimate idioms of discrimination surreptitiously take hold of hearts and minds.

Today however, in the era of globalisation, the customary antinomy of frontlines, backyards has become uncoupled from its historic relay systems. These are no longer easily correlated with divisions of labour or leisure or allocated into public and private realms. Under the impact of new information technologies, homepages link frontline struggles against global concentrations of capital into no less global but dispersed networks of backyard support. The effective governance of the state goes transnational, while the electronic body politic runs subterranean power lines through the common culture of complaint that the loss of 'sovereignty' provokes amongst its fractious citizenries. Contraflows of population and ideas, from East to West, from South to North disrupt the old Eurocentric geographies; new frontiers of 'backlash' are set up against this 'alien' traffic, along beaches and waterfronts, in university faculties and housing estates, wherever the empty fortress of the racist imagination feels threatened and demands a re-concentration of autochthony around the policing of border camps.

For all these reasons we find ourselves living in an uncertain era where the boundaries between state and civil society, local and global, blur, and one community's frontline increasingly runs through another's backyard. Which is what the then Tory deputy prime minister Mr Heseltine discovered recently when he looked out of the conservatory of his country seat and found a profane alliance of new age travellers and ex-miners digging up his front lawn in order to expose the fact that underneath lay a rich seam of coal suitable for exploitation by open-cast mining, a cause otherwise dear to Mr Heseltine's heart.

When a frontline invades a backyard, where what was once a backyard has become a frontline, we have a political borderland that cuts across existing territories of identification. We can glimpse these borderlands taking shape in certain new coalitions of concern around issues of health, education and the environment. And we can see them emerging in the work of many contemporary cultural tricksters who have learned to live and work on both sides of the race, gender or class line.

The African-American artist David Hammons is a good example of this. In his work he uses materials that are part of the detritus of cocacolonial consumerism, but are also redeemed by their usage within the vernacular culture of AfroAmerica: grease, chicken parts, hair, bottle tops, beer cans. Using these elements he builds art in public yet interstitial spaces in a way that relies on the 'now you see it, now you don't' puns of the African trickster. His 'bottle trees' use empty beer bottles to transform the Ailanthus (otherwise known as the 'poverty tree') into a statement about the double-edged nature of intoxication in black culture. Dawoud Bey describes the context of this work in the following terms:

> Walk through Harlem any given day and you will see his work, the work he does for people who cannot go to SoHo and gallery shop. The people that he knows. The people that he comes from. Bottles stuck on top of bare branches protruding from the ground. From vacant lots and cracks and crevices in the sidewalk, Hammons transforms them to

create visual music, something to smile about in an environment that doesn't offer a lot in the way of jokes. But those cheap wine bottles have touched Black lips, lips looking for a cheap way out of a predicament whose ultimate cost is very high.[2]

Liminality can be creative of genuinely new idioms of cultural contestation; yet there is always a residual suspicion that the cultural trickster is simply trying to have it both ways; in the case of black artists, it must be a great temptation to make a lot of money by selling work to rich white collectors through the gallery circuit, whilst at the same time doing just enough 'public art' to retain some street cred with the black community. Certainly there are just as many instances where the effects of marginality implode to generate aggressive or self-destructive forms of escapism, and where technologies of chemical and ideological 'transcendence' combine forces to create a habitus of magical omnipotence fatally attractive to all those who are losing out in the struggle to 'get a life'.

What makes Hammons' work so different is his alertness to the other side of the story, its centrality to his appropriation of the dadaist gesture. You will not find the same thing happening in Britpop art! There is no critical sense in 'Sensation' of what is going down in housing estates the length and breadth of de-industrialised Britain; only, in some cases, a seductive, but hollow mimetics of despair. The artist cross-dresses as a bother-boy to play at king of the castle; just as their opposite numbers, bald as new born babies, and still wearing dungarees to go with their hob-nailed boots, as they flex their muscles to prove that the others are the real mummies' boys; meanwhile, under bridges, along canals, on the walls of a hundred derelict factories, you can read the signs of races, nations and classes that do not feature on the official maps of new Britain drawn by new Labour, but which offer another, sometimes more, sometimes less, hopeful set of directions as to where we might be heading.

The allegiances of these borderlands are as mobile as their location. They do not fit within any neat concordance of political and cultural aspiration. Those who argue for their incorporation in a 'stakeholder polity' have first to deal with a paradox partly of their own making. The language of barricades, mass mobilisations and 'they shall not pass' seems to belong to another era, another kind of urban space, where large crowds were more than a collective pose for the mass media, and indeed were direct agents of the historical process. Nevertheless even in a so-called post-modern world, where political protest rooted in stable communities of local interest has supposedly been rendered obsolete by more dispersed, individualised and global networks of affiliation, the most obdurate struggles continually break out in and around the frontdoors/backyards of whatever is called home. As one Bangladeshi community leader in East London put it to me:

I can surf the Internet, I can phone my relatives around the world, but

I am afraid sometimes to go out of my front door in the morning to go round the corner to the paper shop in case I get attacked by a gang of racist thugs, who happen to live across the road.[3]

3. See Sally Westwood and John Williams (eds), *Imagining the City*, Routledge, London 1997.

It is tempting to resolve this paradox by relocating its terms within an updated version of the binaries and boundaries of the past. But it really is wishful thinking to believe that the masses, as historically constituted, live on in the presence of the street massives. That new world, for all its echoes of proletarian combination, really does dance to different anthems. The fact is that the historical compromise between local working-class communities and the capitalist city has been shaken up beyond any easy resettlement, as much by the feminisation of immigrant labour from the so-called Third World, as by the deconstruction of contemporary forms of masculinity and manual labour in the West; and this in a way which compromises national and class boundaries just as much as gendered and racialised ones.[4]

4. Phil Cohen, 'Beyond the community romance', *Soundings* 5, Lawrence & Wishart, London 1997.

There are, of course, a range of responses to this complication of political landscape in the 1990s. There are those who celebrate the new uncertainty principles, who exploit the luxuriant phenomenology of fragmentation and fluidity for their own narcissistic purposes, and fetishise the borderlands as sites of cultural or political transgression; en route the migrant and asylum-seeker, the unemployed and the down-and-out: all those in need of the security and safety afforded by a settled existence and full rights of citizenship guaranteed by the state, are often transfigured into a kind of nomadic postmodern hero by those who take all that for granted, and whose sense of possibility is confined only by the power of their own imaginations and of the institutions in whose pockets they live.

And then there are those who dig in around entrenched positions of militancy, draw an inflexible Maginot line of race, class or gender division, confident on their side of shared roots and final victory; they have more in common than they would like to recognise with the cultural conservatives who canvass a return to familial or communitarian values, and who confuse the universal need to maintain firm boundaries – between where selves begin and others end – with policies of self-containment which draw the lines of discrimination under one's own feet.

The present debate between postmodernism and various kinds of essentialism has degenerated into a slanging match between the advocates of healthy happy hybridity, on one side, and the defenders of pathological purity on the other. There are many, myself among them, who feel that the terms of this debate are absurd, but who are also demoralised by the onward march of particularisms; for this has happened at a time when the larger stories that once promised liberation are themselves indicted as part of the tyranny of Western Reason, rendered complicit with imperial humanisms and scientisms which turned out to owe more to the logic of fairy stories than any properly experimental procedure. To abandon these omniscient vantage points would seem to leave us with the insuperable problem of how to sustain a struggle of long duration without the support of long-term principles of hope and with only the vacuous and febrile theoreticisms of the postmodern turn to comfort us. Yet is there also a possibility that, in the very act of tracing the unravelling of these fairy tales, we might discover the threads of a rather different conversation with hope?

We are all looking for story lines uncomplicit in dreams for an altogether better world that turned nightmare; we are equally desperate for political movements uncompromised by surrender to reality-principles that offer only more of the same to those who do not even have walk-on parts in the making of history. If we are to regain a sense of political ambition less freighted with failed hopes and given that we cannot start by going back to any kind of ideological foundation myth, we have no alternative but to practise the kind skepsis that both Gramsci and Rilke, in their different ways, recommended. To begin afresh, in the struggle to make over whatever is within reach of the individual imagination into some more commonly habitable universe of discourse, they both suggested you had to undertake an inventory of cultural or spiritual resource.

At a time dominated by the facile rhetorics of rejuvenation associated with new Labourism and the rebranding of Britain as 'cool Britannia', such a poetics of political beginning, of 'making over', or even 'making good' is inevitably risky; its costs and benefits are not likely to add up to any simple political calculus. But the move we have to make, from a cultural politics of liminality to a mainstream political culture recentred around what that agenda has added to our sense of what is at stake, cannot be achieved by any other means.

WHO NEEDS AN ISLAND . . .?

One point of reckoning where we can start this inventory is with the historical processes which have shaped the formation of an archipelagic identity for the 'British Isles', rendering it into a multi-ethnic but anglophone society within a unitary state. What has the appeal to 'islishness' added to or subtracted from the sense of being British? How has it worked as a device for assimilating a whole range of nationalities, some 'home grown', some not, within the hegemonic insularities of Englishness? And how have the myths of origin and destiny associated with the Anglo-Saxon island-race story come to contend with the co-existence of rival archipelagos, whose narratives run counter to its imperial design? The Caribbean and Irish island-stories, for example, are a central element in the local intelligence of where we live now.

Until we can answer these questions we cannot begin to estimate what the project of political devolution might inagurate. Nor could we say, with any confidence, whether from the ashes of this disunited unkingdom some version of the British Isles might yet be born which is more than a site for the projection of rival insularities arising from old colonial engagements with the trans-continental discourses of Europe, Asia and Africa.

This line of thought was triggered by seeing a recent advertisement for a brand of coconut rum.[5] This showed a black middle-class couple sitting contentedly in deckchairs, in their own typically English suburban garden, above a caption reading:

5. Much of the argument here is developed in greater detail in Phil Cohen, *Island stories in the making and unmaking of Britain*, CNER, London 1998.

Who needs an island
when you've got a back garden?
Who needs palm trees
when you've got rhododendron?
Who needs the Caribbean
when you've got Malibu?

At first sight the advertisement represents a rather cruel double-take on the aspirations and achievements of the new black British middle class. They are portrayed as having traded their roots radicalism for the comforts of English life-style, whilst continuing to imbibe the essential spirit of black Caribbean identity (courtesy of Malibu). But the ad contains another, more coded set of references addressed to its 'other audience': the white English tourists who visit the Caribbean in search of sun, sea and sexotic experience. They too can now stay at home and savour the taste of black culture in the comfort of their own backyards.

Through its play of substitutions the advertisement invites us to join in a rather curious game of trading places, built around mutual disavowal and false equivalence. The black couple are made to disown a travestied version of their own island culture, in order to guarantee its authenticity as a source of disavowed desire on the part of a white audience whom they in turn displace and represent by proxy. The storyline is ghosted in a double sense; it enables Malibu to cross the racial divide in the name of a 'transcendental consumerism' which blurs all the distinctions that make its appeal possible. Patently, the 'common culture' it proposes is nothing of the sort; for in one case it could only evoke a longing to return home, in order to escape from everyday life in multi-racist Britain; and for the white English it is merely a matter of wanting to escape the vagaries of the British winter. This disjuncture is made seductively easy to swallow. For Malibu is implicitly promoted as a kind of magic potion that dispels racism just as easily as it blows away the rain clouds; it not only relieves black consumers of diasporic angst, but absolves whites of post-imperial guilt. No wonder it makes everyone feel so good.

Yet there is another, more hidden, set of substitutions at work, one that takes us beyond any simple act of 'deconstruction' towards a deeper, more historically-grounded appreciation of what is at stake. The reference to the tropical island paradise trades off and conceals its other less acceptable dimension: that of an island race who set off in small wooden boats to conquer the world and whose rapacious exploits brought the world's

produce to its front parlours and back gardens, and 'made of them a continent entire'. As Derek Walcott said of the English colonial settlers in the
West Indies, they 'helped themselves to these green islands, like olives
from a saucer, munched on the pith, then spat their sucked stones on a
plate, like a melon's black seeds'.[6]

6. Derek Walcott,
Omeros, Faber and
Faber, London 1990.

The island story that the Malibu advertisement does not tell, but
depends on for its special effect, is a strange concatenation of hybridised
ethnicity and racial purity. The burden of my argument is that these are
two sides of the same story, not alternative versions of Britishness.

On one side the island has been a highly efficient device for asserting
Anglo-Saxon racial superiority and for establishing English sovereignty
over the Welsh and Scots under the flag of Britannia, while simultaneously
colonising and pushing the Irish beyond the pale of mainland civilisation.
Yet if Little England needs Wales and Scotland before it can, littorally
speaking, constitute an island at all, the exclusionary terms under which
the English have constructed themselves as a pure-bred island race have
also made them into the backbone of an inclusive, hybridised British
nation. This circle was squared in the claim that the Anglo-Saxon
possessed a uniquely 'islish' propensity to absorb and manage cultural
diversity whilst at the same time making this a mark of superior breeding.
En passant, the Celtic nations are confined to an ethnic periphery (shared
with all those others who merely breed), a periphery that somehow does
not have separate coastal, and hence (according to this archipelagic
doctrine) political, identity.[7]

7. See, for example,
M. Hetcher,
*International
Colonialism – the
Celtic fringe in
British development*,
Routledge, London
1978; and Brendan
Bradshaw and John
Morrill (eds), *The
British Problem*,
Macmillan, London
1996.

Whether the racial peculiarities of the English are traced back to
Teutonic, Trojan or biblical roots, they have always been carefully amalga-
mated with the diverse heritage of an 'island home'; as a result empire
building – either of an internal 'British Empire in Europe' kind or of a
world maritime power – is seen as a natural expression or extention of an
innate and genial multiculturalism. Before we trace the unravelling of this
particular grand narrative, it might be worth considering just what is
entailed in its making.

It may seem self-evident that islands and races are made for one another,
easy accomplices in the projection of self-sufficient sovereignties of every
kind; yet the island is a relative not an absolute category; the notion of land
encompassed by sea is a necessary but not a sufficient, condition; it
requires a further act of circumscription in the mind's eye, some process of
narrative circumnavigation, in order to create an imaginary vantage point
from which sea and landscape can be taken in panoptically as a singular
insular whole.[8]

8. On the island
panopticon see
Abraham Moles and
Elisabeth Rohmer,
*Labyrinthes du
Vecu*, Librarie
Manche, Paris 1982;
see also the discus-
sion in Nicholas
Ruddick, *The
Ultimate Island*,
Greenwood Press,
London 1995; and
Elias Canetti,
Crowds And Power,
Penguin,
Harmondsworth
1981.

The island thus constitutes a peculiar kind of travelling story. Only
when a point is reached that is recognised as marking the beginning, only
when we arrive back at where we first started, do the journey and the story
end. So we have an apparently linear narrative, which turns imperceptibly
in the course of its unfolding into a circularity: a process entirely appro-

priate to its mythopoetic function, which is to create the island as a place of ideal beginnings and happy endings outside time. Yet this utopian paradise also poses problems for an account which has pretensions to travel in unidirectional historical time, in a word, to be a story of nation-building. At this point genealogy has to give way to teleology: a principle of external causation has to be introduced. The island has to be invaded, settled, transformed sometimes by benign forces, sometimes by hostile ones. The invader in this context has an epistemological function, to narrativise causality and to subsume it under rules of consequence. It is at the point where the island story turns into an invasion story that the nation's founding myths become actively racialised.

In terms of that Atlantic archipelago, first named Albion and then the British Isles, the problem of how to unite local kingdoms of perception or survey within some overarching universe of discourse was always the main task of state and nation building. For in literal, cartographic terms, the landmass of Great Britain was far too large and complex to lend credence to its existence as a simple eye-land. Indeed the colonial enterprise owes much of its utopian drive to the quest for an ideal surrogate island state, an Illyria, whose small-scale physical geography would furnish a natural symbol of sovereignty immediately given to the senses, yet still subject to investigation and control by an empire of the mind furnished with fabulous prospects. How else could castaways turn lords of humankind? Or Prospero tame Caliban?[9]

Back home an enormous effort of land and seascaping was required to construct the habitus of an island race from the ground up and render it politically and cultural legible. This patriotic labour of poets, painters, cartographers, farmers, mariners, gardeners, foresters, domestic travellers and foreign tourists began with Gloriana and 'the Sceptred Isle', and reached its zenith in the eighteenth and early nineteenth centuries with the 'discovery' of a romantic coastal sublime to match the longer-established Arcadian interior; this work in turn laid the foundations for an imperial vision which aimed to unite the islands which got to travel – those little Englands constructed as dreams of tropic paradise in the colonies overseas – with the islands that stayed at home – the New Jerusalems that were to be built by freeborn Englishmen amidst the dark satanic mills.[10]

Much has rightly been made of the cultural resistance which this imperial mission evoked amongst both its internal and external colonial subjects. Yet we should not overlook the fact that the physical geography of the British Isles also resisted easy translation into a unifying cultural or political geography. It took the intervention of particular kinds of discourse, specific loco-descriptive strategies, to conform map to territory and naturalise the link, so that by the end of the last century it was possible for little Englanders to say, with neither irony nor anomaly, that they inhabited a small island destined to rule the world.

The island-race story is founded on a paradox. Here is an English nation

9. See for example the discussion in Ernst Bloch, *The Principle of Hope*, Basil Blackwell, Oxford 1986; and Richard Grove, *Green Imperialism*, Cambridge University Press 1995.

10. See Simon Schama, *Memory and Landscape*, HarperCollins, London 1995; Alain Corbin, *The Lure of the Sea*, Polity, Cambridge 1994; Esther Moir, *The Discovery of Britain*, Routledge, London 1964; C.A. Bayly, *The Imperial Meridian*, Longman, London 1989; Stephen Daniels, *Fields of Vision*, Polity, Cambridge 1993.

continually being founded from outside itself, by the advent of strangers from continents overseas. The island story is never *not* an account of its invasion and settlement. How then was it possible to impose a pattern of insular meaning on this constant rupture, and give to the nation a singular over-arching narrative identity?

This was achieved in a number of different but linked ways, all of them designed to establish lines of defence against admitting the 'invaders', who always and already inhabited the citadel of Anglo-islishness, to full civil and narrative rights. The first strategy involved connecting temporal continuity to spatial contiguity; a coastal perimeter was described, threading through cliffs and bays, harbours and ports, estuaries and docklands, to form a bulwark of invented tradition against anything that might erode the nation's political integrity. Here is how Michael O'Shea, at that time press secretary to the Queen, makes the connections:

11. Michael O'Shea, *Maritime England – the Nation's Heritage*, Country Life Books, London 1981. See also, in similar vein, Arthur Bryant, *Freedom's Own Island*, Collins, London 1986; and Christopher Lee, *The Sceptral Isle*, BBC Books, 1997.

> That we have a unique history as a nation never conquered and a democratic political system which is enviably independent is also largely the result of our invincibility, protected as we are by the seas, straits and channels that lie all around us. In social terms the peculiarities of the English way of life are again as much attributable to our isolation on our islands as to any innate and uneasily national characteristics. As a nation we and our ways owe much to the sea.[11]

So here the founding myth of English democracy, the signing of Magna Carta on the 'island' of Runnymede, is inscribed within a wider genealogy of resistance to outside influence. The idea that the islishness of the British constituted a natural bulwark of popular democratic values against foreign tyranny has at least as long a historical provenance as the notion of the freeborn Englishman, and the two are intimately linked.[12] This idea was taken up by the British psychoanalyst D.W. Winnicott, the architect of much post-war thinking about child development and family values, in the following terms:

12. See Linda Colley, *Britons – Forging the Nation*, Pimlico, London 1994; and Hugh Cunningham, 'The Language of Patriotism', in Raphael Samuel (ed), *Patriotism*, Routledge, London 1989.

13. D.W. Winnicott, *Radio Times* 'Interview', September 1956.

> For the development of a democracy, in the sense of a mature society, it seems that it is necessary that there should be some natural geographical boundary for that society. The fact that Great Britain is seabound (except for its relation to Eire) has been very much responsible for the maturity of our societal structure.[13]

Winnicott's definition of political – and emotional – maturity turned on the capacity to integrate or bring into some kind of workable relation many different elements or tendencies within both society and the self. For him the island functions as a symbolic container of conflicts in a way that facilitates their resolution through internal negotiation and settlement. The fact of seaboundedness furnishes a privileged ecology for attracting and nurturing a rich diversity of cultures, while holding them within a common frame. We are thus presented with two articulations of democracy and the island; in the first case they work together to repel outside influence in the name of an organic uniqueness; in the second their interaction actively encourages biopolitical diversity. The same features of British islishness are used to signify national integrity and cultural hybridity. For all the conjunctural tensions between policies of racial exclusion and assimilation, at a deeper level the island story makes it possible to move seamlessly between rhetorics of ethnic and civic nationalism. Little England somersaults into the arms of Great Britain. The circle is squared.

So far we have been dealing with relatively undifferentiated cartographies of the 'island home'. But over the last 150 years the anatomy of insularity has been repeatedly refined.[14] Each point of entry is treated as a potential inroad into the body politic and invested by special custodians who police the ebb and flow of traffic between coast and hinterland, native and foreign shores. Let us note in passing the special role reserved for the docker, the lighterman, the seafarer, the coastguard, as the nation's watchdogs. These 'hearts of oak' are made to function as a sturdy maritime yeomanry dedicated to preserving the natural symbolism of Englishness by both land and sea. It is from their ranks that white labourism was born in campaigns against the 'alien' invasion of Jews, and against the use of 'coolie' labour on British ships. The multiracial communities of lascars, East Africans, Chinese, Jews and Irish who settled and plied their trades and created their disparate 'tiger bays', not only in Cardiff, but in the East End of London, in Glasgow, Hull and Bristol, were always a principal target of exclusionary practice and sometimes, as in the riots of 1919, actual racial violence.[15]

Nevertheless as the movement for colonial independence pressed its claims, and the empire prepared to strike back, the political rhetoric of multicultural containment grew more persuasive, and even diehard imperialists began to use it: Winston Churchill in his story of *The Island Race* (1964), for example argues that the British Isles are:

> very accessible to the invader, whether he comes in peace or war, as pirate or merchant, conqueror or missionary. Those who dwell there are not insensitive to any shift of power, any change of faith, but they give to every practice, every doctrine that comes to it from abroad, its peculiar turn and imprint.[16]

So here the 'invaders' are eventually absorbed within a common mentality and way of life and a deal struck in which sensitivity to difference and change is not allowed to interfere with the rights of the already-indigenous to dictate the terms of settlement. It is this power of assimilation that constitutes the ultimate protection of the island race, rather than sea defences that are all too easily breached. By separating the littoral from the metaphorical boundaries of the nation a second line of defence is created,

14. The painstaking construction of the island race story 'on the ground' through a whole variety of local topographies is a still largely untold story. Most analyses treat the island story as a grand narrative associated exclusively with the heyday of Victorian imperialism and its strategy of dissemination into popular culture. See for example the contributions to John Mackenzie (ed), *Propaganda and Empire*, Manchester University Press 1984; and James Mangan (ed), *Imperial Mentalities*, Manchester University Press 1990.

15. See Laura Tabili, *We Ask for British Justice: workers and racial difference in late imperial Britain*, Cornell University Press, Ithaca, New York 1994.

16. See Winston Churchill, *The Island Race*, Webber and Bower, Exeter 1964.

based on culture, mirroring nature's ways. But what would happen when this too became permeable?

The need to absorb so many different cultural influences within the story of a proud maritime nation, standing alone amidst a sea of foreign troubles, was always going to be a source of anxiety for island-story tellers. There are many who have clung to the natural symbolism of the seabound island, even if, in doing so, they have had to extend its metaphoric scope beyond the realms of credibility. Sir Roy Strong, in his recent *The Story of Britain* (1996), can still assert:

> Britain is an island and that fact is more important than any other in understanding its history. The country was invaded piecemeal by those resilient enough to brave the rough waters of its encircling seas. Because of that difficulty small numbers came and once here they were absorbed into the existing population.[17]

17. Roy Strong, *The Story of Britain*, Hutchinson, London 1996.

In his account, the rites of sea passage magically transform foreign invaders into potential kith and kin by initiating them into the mysteries of a maritime island race. The fact that 'anyone who came, had to make a storm tossed journey in a boat' is for him the key factor. The sea here acts not so much as a barrier, as a filter, a principle of natural selection, weeding out undesirables, and ensuring that only the fittest, those with the physical and moral fibre to survive the voyage, qualify for landing cards. And since only the resilient make it, there is no problem about their assimilation.

The trope of the sea as a purifying agent, decontaminating the body politic, again has a long historical provenance, dating back at least to the *Adventus Saxonum*.[18] Roy Strong gives a contemporary, neo-Darwinian twist to the tale by implying that once the sea no longer serves as nature's own system of immigration control, other measures, of the same order, will be needed to sort out those who are to sink or swim on land. The state will have to intervene to shore up a second bio-political line of defence, mirroring the cleansing action of Britannia's seas.

18. For a discussion of the Adventus Saxonum, see J. McDougall, *Racial Myths in English History*, Routledge, London 1982.

Here we can see how the island story turns into a fully fledged invasion-story when and wherever the symbolic interaction of sea and landscape becomes racialised and draws a line of discrimination between 'nurturant' immigrants who go on to become model minorities, and 'alien invaders' who wash up like human refuse on the beach to form a parasitic race apart. Two 'waves' breaking on very different shore lines.[19]

One of the difficulties of constructing island race-ism around a system of imagined coastal defences is that once this 'bulwark' is penetrated, the invasion alarm bells go off. One way of stopping the narrative from being continually inundated by 'alien floods' is to let the sea benignly 'invade' the hinterland, imposing its own armature of meaning on what would otherwise be an amorphous space. Rivers, lakes, sea birds, even the wind, provide 'reminders' of the coast. The process may be humanised by having settlers, with 'salt in their blood' carry sea-bred sensibilities with them as

19. For a discussion of these two positions as articulated within codes of breeding, see Phil Cohen, 'The Perversions of Inheritance' in Cohen and Bains (eds), *Multi Racist Britain*, Macmillan 1988.

they move inland and establish the architecture of a settled polity. The two ideas are often combined, as in this evocation of racial memory by Francis Brett Young in a long narrative poem celebrating the defiant stand-alone islishness of the British in 1940.

> yet remember
> how these were ever bred in cognisance
> of the sea's neighbourhood: there is no brook
> of midmost Mercia but can taste the brine
> of Trent or Severn, ...
> no native blood
> unstirred by those salt savours that beguiled
> Celt, Saxon, Dane, and Norman to forsake
> their homely garths and fields and to explore
> the mysterious oceans.[20]

20. Francis Brett Young, *The Island*, Methuen, London 1944.

In reality, until the mid-nineteenth century and the growth of the seaside as a popular resort, those who lived and worked around the coastal perimeter had little intercourse with inhabitants of the interior. Many populations who worked along the shorelines, or on the sea itself, were officially regarded as a dangerous race apart: smugglers, wreckers, pirates, potential traitors to the patriotic cause.[21] Their 'conversion' into back-bones of the nation coincides with a process of 'turning inwards' in the island-race story, a symbolic turning away from the sea, to build a further line of defence against the stranger within.

21. See Corbin, *op. cit.*; and also John Rule, *Albion's People*, Longman, London 1992.

The midsummer dream that has cast the most decisive spell over what it means to be forever England, takes place in a wood, out of sight or sound of the seashore. The great romantic landscapes that have been painted of England's green and pleasant land have tended to treat rivers, lakes and even shorelines as pastoral devices. Wordsworth's valley of contentment all 'blinded holiness of earth and sky made for itself, and happy in itself perfect contentment, unity entire' is a paradigm of this landlocked Arcadia. It celebrates the fact that in the process of settlement the world of *The Tempest* has been left forever behind.

Within this sheltered environment it then becomes possible to create little havens of insularity, localised little Englands that mimic the functions of coastal inhabitation, without its risks. Rivers, lakes, fountains, rock pools, even sandy beaches no longer function as reminders of the sea but are pastoralised and miniaturised for local implantation in the English garden. It is above all in the cultivation of gardens and the picturesque country scene that this vision of a harmonising, all-embracing aesthetic of Englishness is most precisely landscaped. And here, in the careful arrange-ment of contrasting views and prospects, we find the same principles of controlled variation that are at work in the multicultural rendition of the island nation. James Thompson, author of 'The Seasons' (as well as of 'Rule Britannia') endorsed Pope's preference for:

Not chaos like together crush'd and bruised
but as the world, harmoniously confused
where Order in Variety we see
and where, tho all things differ, all agree.[22]

22. Quoted in Michael Andrew, *The Search for the Picturesque*, Scholar Press, Aldershot 1990.

This classical principle of *concordia discors*, the harmonising of discords, runs like a thread through all the arts and sciences of English assimilationism. Its ruling formula was simple: the English provided the order, the others provided the variety. Yet this thin green storyline was made to be breached; its telling almost demanded a succession of invaders moving 'in waves' into the hinterland of Middle England threatening to 'swamp' its most precious redoubts, crushing and bruising native sensibilities. Much of the writing of Englishness in this century has been concerned with exploring the liminalities that ensue when the littoral defences of the nation give way to more complex and metaphorical strategies of insulation, and the chaos that ensues when these symbolic frontlines and backyards no longer furnish adequate controls on the process of cultural miscegenation, so that wilder forms of hybridity take over.[23]

23. For a discussion of hybridity as a theme in English letters see Howard Weibrot, *Britannia's Issue*, Cambridge University Press 1994; Robert Young, *Colonial Desire*, Routledge, London 1995.

In the late 1930s Edward Upward, a close friend of Christopher Isherwood and W.H. Auden, published a short story called 'The Railway Accident'. It describes a journey undertaken by some typical 'well-bred' English upper-middle-class types to the country for a weekend house-party, a journey which begins in familiar territory, but which then goes increasingly off the rails as the underlying violence and madness of the situation comes to the surface. The 'Mortmere Express' is full of soldiers, territorials belonging to Colonel Moxon's English Rifles, whose boisterous behaviour gets out of hand as they break down the bulkhead separating the first and third class compartments. The narrator's companion is obsessed with making a detailed map of the country they are travelling through in order to convince himself that they are not heading for disaster.

As the story and the journey progress it becomes clear that the map is not the territory and the territory is most definitely not the map. The 'Mortmere Express', a figment of the narrator's imagination, is following in the tracks of a similar train that ran into a collapsed tunnel, several years previously, killing everyone on board. No one is in a position to avert a repetition of the disaster. However at the last minute the narrator and his companion manage to jump clear. They find their way to Mortmere Manor, where an elaborate game of hide and seek has been arranged as the centre piece of the weekend party. The game also starts to go off the rails, bringing to the surface the sadism underlying its civilities. It too ends in an act of violence which no one is able to avert.

Here is Upward's description of the garden at Mortmere where the game is played out:

The arum colocasia, lupines, lentils, the pomegranate sycamore, date palms, yew, beech and privet, fenugreek, meloukhia, the Acacia

Fainesiana, carob tree, mimosa habbas, lemon verbena, nasturtium, vole and lily snakes hung from the elm branches, pigeons rose from the black antennae of leaves startled by the engine of a car. Across the water of the sun-white marshes, alligator fishermen punted their raft. Blue tiled houses had grown like bushes out of the ground ... Odour of chimes of croquet hoops, tango of views of choirboys through the rustling privet ...

The controlled multicultural harmonies of the English garden, with its carefully arranged interplay of exotically named plants designed to set off by contrast the superior order of the native bloom, here takes on a more ominous tone. Real and imaginary flowers and landscapes jostle side by side, croquet lawns run down to alligator swamps. Even the image of organic community takes on a threatening wildness, 'blue tiled houses growing like bushes out of the ground'. The signifiers of old Englishness, which should have provided a safe haven from the disruptions of modernity, figure an even more discomforting universe, a world which has tipped over into madness.

The madness is still with us, but it has been sanitised, or rather multi-culturalised. It is, for example, present in a recent advertisement for Kew Gardens. This image is a postmodern come-on in an even more cynical,

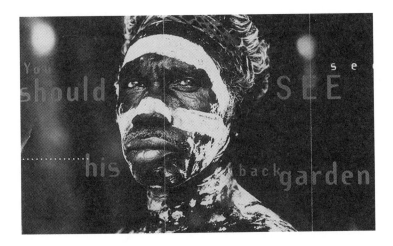

and knowing fashion than the Malibu advertisement. Native Australians did not customarily have gardens in the English sense; they had symbolic landscapes (dreaming) that were invisible to white settlers, because fashioned as reticular or nomadic spaces; there are no neatly ordered classifications of fauna and flora as found in the botanical gardens at Kew. What the advertisement invites us to do is finally to misrecognise what escaped the grasp of the Victorian collectors of human and animal species: namely that 'the authentic essence' of aboriginal culture for Westerners is fixed precisely by its invisibility, by its inert resistance to scrutiny from any standpoint other than its own. This culture can safely be transplanted to Kew Gardens, precisely because it can be rooted in the principle of *corncordia discors*, to underpin that quiet sense of superiority, that marks the English imagination at home with itself. The advertisement invites us to collude with the multiculturalist project as knowing insiders to its particular language-game. That is how it proposes to let us off the hook of post-colonial guilt.

Yet by the beginning of the twentieth century, science and technology were making such manoeuvres redundant. Invisible waves, waves which transmitted populations and ideas from one side of the planet to another, but did not break on any shore, were melting everything that had seemed so solid about the white cliffs of Dover and the gardens of Middle England into diasporic air.[24]

24. See Gillian Beer, *Arguments with the Past*, Routledge, London 1991. Also Jonathan Raban, *Coasting*, Picador, London 1986.

Ironically it was the materialisation of this threat, in a real not imagined war of the worlds, which helped temporarily to re-stabilise the evanescent sense of English identity. Suddenly unified by a common threat from aerial bombardment in World War II the island home was reinvented as a nation under arms. Dover became a new front line, under bombardment from German guns. The Battle of Britain was a sea battle fought in the skies, while the population of the home counties watched from their snug ensconsements in the gardens and allotments of Southern England. Graham Swift brilliantly captures this moment, in *Waterland* (1978), when a whole range of insularities which at one level has been made redundant, is at another being given a new lease of life.

> In the late Summer of 1940, while Hitler sets up shop in Paris and makes invasion plans, while over southern skies history inscribes itself in white scrolls and provides ample material for the legends of the future, he [the narrator] rummages amongst the books his mother left behind and embarks on the two volumes of Hereward the Wake. While the inhabitants of London and other large cities are forced to take refuge within the solid fabric of air raid shelters and underground stations, he takes refuge in the fanciful fabric of Kingsley's yarn in which in misty fenland settings history merges with fiction, fact gets blurred with fable.[25]

25. Graham Swift, *Waterland*, Heinemann, London 1983.

Who better than Hereward, that standard bearer of Anglo-Saxon liberties, who single-handedly defied the Norman Conquest from his marshy fastness on the isle of Ely, to represent the mongrel race in their darkest and finest hour, as they stood alone against the threat of fascist invasion?

Dunkirk and the Battle of the Britain were the last moments in which the association of physical and political geography could be unproblematically sustained. By 1945 Britain no longer ruled the waves, neither the airwaves, nor the sea. All the more reason then to fear that Britons, whose ancient liberties had once been guaranteed by naval power, might in their turn become 'enslaved'.

It is against this background that we have to understand how Enoch Powell reconstructed the island-race story.[26] The issue he addressed was no longer how such a small country got to make such a big empire but, on the contrary, how little England could survive the onslaught of a succession of world historical forces: European fascism, Soviet Communism, US coca-colonialism and immigration from the ex-colonies, by somehow remaining herself. Although Powellism is often read as the last gasp of imperial island race-ism, it is more accurate to see it as an attempt to erase that whole history and get back to some pristine pre-colonial founding moment of British Islishness. As Powell put it:

26. See Jonathon Rutherford, *Forever England*, Lawrence & Wishart, London 1997.

> ... at the heart of our vanished empire, amidst the fragments of its demolished glory, the British are able to find, like one of her own oak trees, standing and growing, the sap still rising from her ancient roots to meet the spring, England herself, the continuity of her existence unbroken when looser connections which had linked her with distant continents and strange race fell away.

It is certainly true that when dockers from all over the East End of London marched in support of Enoch Powell, in 1968, following his 'rivers of blood' speech, they imagined themselves to be protesting against a tide of history which was not only bringing ex-colonial subjects up river, to land on their doorsteps, but was sweeping their own livelihoods away, in the opposite direction, down river, to the container port of Tilbury – where, of course, the *Empire Windrush* had docked twenty years before. In fact the frontlines of immigration control had already shifted invisibly, under their feet, and into an altogether different realm where a new racist discourse was was already in place. The immigrants the dockers were worried about were no longer waiting meekly at the dock gates for their permits to land, but were threatening to drop, like predatory birds or avenging angels, from the skies around Heathrow.

Salman Rushdie captured what was at stake in the opening chapter of his 1988 book *The Satanic Verses* in which two of the passengers find themselves in free-fall over Southern England, without a parachute, when the plane carrying them and other immigrants from the Indian subcontinent explodes as it crosses the English channel. Rushdie comments on the way the medium has itself changed the diasporic message:

> Up there is airspace. In that soft imperceptible field which had been made possible by the century, and which thereafter, made the century possible, becoming one of its defining locations, the place of movement and war, the planet shrinker and power vacuum, most insecure and transitory of zone, illusory, discontinuous, metamorphic – because when you throw everything up in the air anything becomes possible, wayupthere at any rate changes took place in delirious actors which would have gladdened the heart of old Mr Lamark – under extreme environment pressure new characteristics were acquired.[27]

27. Salman Rushdie, *The Satanic Verses*, Viking, London 1988.

REVISIONS

Something happens to an island story when it turns its back on the sea and walls itself up in a garden; when waves no longer break against shores, when the slow tug of tides and siltings re-shaping land are no longer available as metaphors of human trade and traffic, the natal attractions of the 'island home' have to seek other roots. Many people retreat into new technologies of insularity: the monadology of the motor car, the solipsism of the skin-encapsulated ego, the narcissism of minor differences organised around physical appearance and style. And in these new conditions island race-ism also flourishes, albeit of a more mobile and individualistic kind, but one which nevertheless still gets under the skin and hurts.[28]

28. For a discussion of the 'postmodern framing' of contemporary racism, see Ali Rattansi and Sally Westwood (eds), *Racism, Modernity and Identity: on the Western Front*, Polity, Cambridge 1994.

Postwar Caribbean settlement in Britain, with its complex and shifting articulation of different island-stories, of Jamaica and Trinidad, Barbados, St Lucia and Grenada, was an unprecedented event that occurred at a major geopolitical turning point. At the very moment at which Britain was being converted into an aircraft carrier for the new United States World Empire, a travelling island-story landed on these shores that brought home everything that had been repressed in its self-aggrandisement as a white Atlantic archipelago.[29]

29 Travelling island stories (both Anglo-Saxon and Caribbean) are a central motif in the construction of white and black Atlanticism, but have received little attention from cultural theorists. See, for instance, Paul Gilroy, *The Black Atlantic*, Verso, London 1994.

The central role played by the Caribbean in the Anglo-Saxon imagination stems from the fact that its island topographies offered a model of coherence entirely lacking from the narrative landscaping of Britishness; seen from afar, the Antilles possessed an archipelagic integrity that had mysteriously got lost in the pursuit of England's own dream of imperial expansion, and which could only be recovered at second-hand, via boys, own adventure stories featuring little Englanders who ran away to sea and got shipwrecked on some tropical island shore.[30]

30. See Patrick Brantliger, *The Rules of Darkness*, Polity, Cambridge 1994; and Keith Carpenter, *Desert Isles and Pirate_Isles*, Frankfurt 1984.

But when the adventure trail ran the other way it was quite another story. When the *Empire Windrush* landed at Tilbury it recapitulated a history the English did not want to recognise, or to remember in themselves: the other 'darker' side of their island-race story; the slavery that had founded these 'other' islands as colonial domains and in which rites of sea passage take on a quite different meaning. Above all what the English did not want to see was the process of alienation from island roots that was required for the formation of an Afro-Caribbean or Black British identity capable of withstanding the rigours of white racism. Grace Nichols movingly evokes this process in her poem 'Island Man':

Morning
and island man wakes up
to the sound of blue surf
in his head
the steady breaking and wombing

wild seabirds
and fishermen pushing out to sea
the sun surfacing defiantly

from the east
of his small emerald island
he always comes back groggily groggily

Comes back to sands
of a grey metallic soar
to surge of wheels
in dull North circular roar
muffling muffling
his crumpled pillow waves
island man heaves himself
another London day.[31]

One of the central paradoxes in the formation of this new identity lay in the fact that it drew on forms of US black urbanism (most notably its street cultures) in a way that accelerated the comprehensive destruction of the Caribbean island culture in its post-colonial diaspora.[32] For example, the functions of the crossroads – as a liminal space where young men learnt the verbal arts of tricksterism from one another – were subsumed under a vernacular street-code to create a new frontline against racism, while the role of the yard (where women used to rule and regulate codes of behaviour) became increasingly privatised. Yardies may be home-boys but the territories they define are most definitely not domestic ones.[33]

As an example of the mappings that resulted from this mutation, consider the image of frontlines produced by a roots-radical black community organisation in London during the 1980s. The bisection of the

31. Quoted in A. Donnel (ed), Caribbean Writing, Routledge, London 1996.

32. See A. Rojo, The Repeating Island – the Caribbean and the Post Modern, Duke University Press, Raleigh, North Carolina 1992.

33. See Roger Abrahams, The Man-of-Words in the West Indies, John Hopkins Press, Baltimore, Maryland 1983.

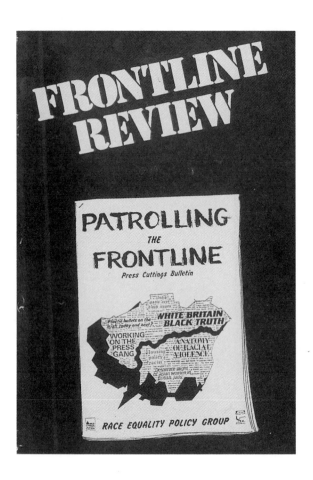

metropolis by the Thames is used to suggest an absolute epistemological rupture in 'regimes of truth'. It is a tendentious frontispiece because the assumed racial binarisms, the evocation of a 'North/South divide' to articulate the image of 'two nations', just does not accord with the complex imbrications of space and race to be found in the post-colonial city. Old Father Thames, ex-multicultural waterfront, ex-artery of empire, ex-white dockland, now bridges the discontinuities in black experience through the very flux of images which it provokes.

This shifting geography has been brilliantly evoked by Fred D'Aguiar in his poem about the river in 'British Subjects':

> I saw these waves
> roping off into strand
> that combine to make a fat rope
> breaking on mud banks and turning pebbles
> . . .
> But the strands formed ropes of their own
> and before I could name what they were
> the ingenious head to which they were plaited

reared up from the tide, widening rings
that marked new heights on the South Bank

. . .

Right then Marley start to skank
his big steps threatened to make the water
break its banks, Barrier or no barrier
this was the dance of the warrior
the more he stamped the lower in the water he sank
until his dreadlocks returned to the waves I mistook
for plaits doing and undoing themselves.[34]

34. Fred D'Aguiar, *British Subjects*, Bloodaxe, 1993.

Through the special alchemy of 'dread', the iconic figure of Marley is transformed into a river-god, the street sounds of reggae are transmuted into an elemental tidal force, and the rastaman's locks merge with waves that Britannia no longer rules.

It has in fact been left to a few caribbean poets: E.A. Markham, Grace Nichols, D'Aguiar and, most famously, Derek Walcott, to reinvent the island story and demonstrate the continued pertinence of its cultural geography.

In Walcott's poetics, the island is transformed from a natural symbol of insularity and particularism into a concrete universal, a site where slaves and castaways learn to throw off the yoke of dereliction 'abandon dead metaphors' and write

Verse crisp as sand, clear as sunlight
Cold as the curled wave, ordinary
as a tumbler of island water.

He urges them to use a vernacular made up of:

the soft vowels of inlets
the pastures of ports
the litany of islands
the rosary of archipelagoes
Anguilla, Antigua
Virgin of Guadaloupe

As his island story has taken on ever-wider archipelagic resonance so it becomes an image of the poet's own homeric vocation to map diaspora:

At the end of the sentence, rain will begin.
At the rain's edge, a sail.

Slowly the sail will lose sight of islands;
into a mist will go the belief in harbours
of an entire race.

The ten years war is finished.
Helen's hair, a grey cloud.
Troy a white ashpit
by the drizzling sea.

The drizzle tightens like the strings of a harp.
A man with clouded eyes picks up the rain
and plucks the first line of the Odyssey.[35]

35. Derek Walcott, *Collected Poems, 1948-84*, Faber and Faber, London 1985.

This is a poetics that uses the island as a singularity, a butterfly attractor, continually precipitating local/global patterns of change. It offers a chaotic counterpoint to the classical principles of *concordia discors*, a way of making over the artificial 'enthropic' paradises created first by colonialism and then by the tourist industry into a more habitable universe.

The Irish also do not inhabit an island of their own making; as an offshore colony of the British Isles, and latterly divided by an artificial internal land border that set in motion sectarian insularities on both sides, Ireland could only be circumnavigated by equally impossible strategies of narrative closure. From the point of view of Anglo-islishness, the scandal of the Catholic claim to 'home rule' was precisely that a united Ireland demanded the same fictive concord between political history and physical geography, national identity and coastal integrity that the English had already monopolised for the purposes of their own internal colonisation of mainland Britain. Equally the embarassment of Protestant Unionism was that it exposed the fraudulent nature of the cartography of Englishness upon which the union was based.[36]

36. See for example Fintan O'Toole, *The Lie of the Land – Irish Identities*, New Island Books, Dublin 1998; and Lawrence McCaffrey, *The Irish Question: Two centuries of Conflict*, University of Kentucky Press, Lexington, Kentucky 1995.

In his poem 'Parable Island',[37] Seamus Heaney has used the whole colonial problematic of the island-story, as explored by William Golding in *Lord of the Flies,* to map out the intrasigence of positionalities that flows from it, commenting sardonically about the Irish case:

37. Seamus Heaney, *The Haw Lantern*, Faber and Faber, London 1987.

Although they are an occupied nation
and their only border is an inland one
they yield to nobody in their belief
that the country is an island

Part of the problem is that there is no agreed correspondence between territory and map. As a result:

To find out where he stands the traveller
has to keep listening – since there is no map
which draws the line he knows he must have crossed

Yet the quest for some fixed Archimedean vantage point from which to accomplish the subterranean reconstruction of the island remains fraught with contradiction and counterfeit hope:

Meanwhile the forked tongued natives keep repeating
prophecies they pretend not to believe
about a point where all names converge
underneath the mountain and where (some day)
they are going to start to mine the ore of truth.

for after all
    you can't be sure that parable is not
    at work already retrospectively
    like the subversives and collaborators
    always vying with a fierce possessiveness
    for the right to set 'the island story' straight

Heaney's ironic distancing from 'the Irish question' is legendary. He seems to see the panoptic vision required to Irish-islishness as part of the problem rather than a solution. In another poem in the same collection he writes of one of the nation's key founding myths:

The land sustaining us seemed to hold firm
Only when we embraced it in extremis
All I believe that happened there was vision.[38]

38. Heaney, *op. cit.*

The vision is sacred, not profane. But religious quests for an isle of the blest have long been instruments of colonial conquest. It is no coincidence that St Brendan was patron saint of the Hanseatic League! In this context Heaney can only hope that the dream of an 'island homecoming' for the Irish identity will be realised by somehow circumventing the extremist tendencies associated with more littoral forms of territorial assertion. Elsewhere he voices the hope that the island 'will disappear by aggrandisement' in the sense of being subsumed under wider, and less insular frames of political and cultural reference. In this way he seeks to outwit the Hegelian dialectic of 'sublation' which has been hijacked by the nationalists. Heaney's project is perhaps not such a far cry from Walcott's after all: the transformation of the post colonial island from a bulwark of inward looking roots radicalism to a butterfly attractor of human affiliations that are both more generous and more outward looking in scope.

MAKING OVER: TOWARDS A POETICS OF POLITICAL BEGINNING

In literature and the arts we are thus beginning to see the emergence of more hopeful ways of circumnavigating islands, reconnecting backyards to frontlines in ways which open up a more constructive conversation between private hope and public need, and perhaps pointing towards an archipelagic vision which is more than a simple restatement of British Islishness. But what lessons does this imaginative achievement have for the much more daunting task of reconstructing our present political culture?

NIMBY (Not In My Back yard) is often characterised as the reactionary face of local insularities, the voice of the little people against the big guns of corporate capitalism and against the global city state. Certainly it is often a way for disparate groups which have been marginalised in the process of urban regeneration to combine to put themselves back on the political map. But does it always have to take this abreactive form?[39]

A story from the East End of London is instructive. In 1936 Moseley's British Union of Fascists proposed to march through the heart of the Jewish community in Whitechapel at a time of rising antisemitism throughout East London. The Moseleyite action provoked a counter mobilisation from left and anti-fascist organisations, which was also supported by sections of the local labour movement. The organising slogan was 'They Shall Not Pass'. It was to be a trial of political strength, with national as well as local implications, and things came to a head in the famous battle of Cable Street, where the BUF were finally stopped.

At that time there lived near Cable Street a working-class family, who were well known for their antisemitism. Some members of the family had supported restrictive practices to prevent Jews from being taken on in the East End manual trades. The younger members had been involved in street brawls with the local Jewish gang. It might have been anticipated that they would welcome Moseley's intervention. But not a bit of it. Like many East Enders, then and since, they were fiercely patriotic in both a local and a national sense. They regarded fascism as a foreign ideology and Moseley's march as an invasion of their territory. On the day of the march, the entire family stationed themselves on top of one of the Jewish houses overlooking Cable Street. They spent their time ripping the slates off the roof and hurling them down onto the heads of the Blackshirts, yelling: 'They may be Yids, but they're our bloody Yids'. In this way they managed simultaneously to attack Jewish property and protect Jewish lives, making their area an exclusion zone for fascism, whilst at the same time asserting their claims as an imaginary ruling class to exercise a form of quasi-colonial jurisdiction over its 'native' inhabitants.

The crossing of this famous frontline by a poetics of the backyard opens up a space of representation that goes beyond both; it not only deconstructs a privileged political mythology of political mobilisation, but indicates the impure resources of meaning that may be set somewhat stealthily in motion behind the subjects' own back in 'a good cause' by actions that otherwise proceed from 'a bad motivation'. Isn't this kind of political tricksterism perhaps what Marx had in mind when he said that 'History invariably proceeds by its bad side'?

One final story may help to illustrate a poetics of political beginning.[40] Mrs Ntolo came to London from the Cameroons in the 1960s, and now lives in a council house on the Becontree Estate, Dagenham. This is a traditional area of white working-class settlement, close to Ford's. Mrs Ntolo

39. See Phil Cohen, *Home Rules – some reflections of racism and nationalism in everyday life,* CNER Monograph, London 1994.

40. Desiree Ntolo, *The Sacred and the Profane,* CNER, London 1994.

belongs to the Essene Community, a group of black Jews who settled in Africa after the fall of the first Temple, and who have been practising a unique syncretic form of Judaism ever since. Part of the requirement of her religion is that certain observances, such as ritual purification and the burning of mourning bands, should be carried out in an oracle, built on especially consecrated ground outside the house, in a way which allows the observant to be in physical contact with the earth. In Africa there is no problem with building the oracle. The word is put around the village that it will be built on such and such a day and everyone puts aside some time to help. It is built of mud and straw, and the structure is made to last for several generations. As Mrs Ntolo discovered, putting up such a structure in your own backyard in England is not a straightforward undertaking.

THE ORATORY

When she wrote to the Planning Department explaining at length her reasons for wanting to put up this structure, and why it had to be built of these materials, she at first got an enthusiastic response. The Planning Department even rang the local papers to tell them all about it. But when the Man from Housing arrived on the scene it was a very different story. They couldn't have their tenants putting up mud huts all over the place. What would people think? The neighbours had already complained. After all, this was Essex not Africa. Why couldn't she assimilate like other people? If she had been white, it might be different, but if they allowed her to go ahead it would set a bad example to other black tenants. Anyway, they had had a look at it and it was definitely a dangerous structure, unfit for human habitation.

It did not stop at insults. The council sent in workmen to knock the Oracle down. They had quite a job because they did not understand the principles of its construction. From the reports they thought it must be a flimsy temporary structure (what else is a hut?) that would fall down at the drop of a pickaxe, whereas in fact the oracle was built to last for generations.It took an earth-digger, two bulldozers, and ten men working for a week to complete the demolition.

The press ran the story, ignoring the religious and cultural politics of the issue, and presenting it as a bad case of homesickness: Mrs Ntolo was putting up a mud hut to remind her of her happy childhood in the Cameroons. No doubt the intention of this 'human angle' was to win sympathy, but the effect was the opposite. Hate mail poured in suggesting that she be helped to go back to the jungle where she belonged.

Meanwhile the council decided to take Mrs Ntolo to court, to get a possession order to evict her from the house, as well as an injunction preventing her from erecting a similar structure again. The judge was not amused. The council had behaved outrageously. It was the right of every freeborn Englishman – and in this case, woman – to practise their religion in the privacy of their own home. The garden was still a private space and the Oracle was interfering with no one. In no way could it be considered a dangerous structure. Still, you had to take account of local feelings. Mrs Ntolo could rebuild the Oracle, using the original materials, provided the structure was encased in concrete. So on the outside it would look like a modern European type of building, while on the inside it would still be an African mud hut. That way everyone would be happy. Mrs Ntolo could carry out her religious observances, and the rest of the world would not be offended.

This masterpiece of legal equivocation around 'race relations' was not however the end of the story. Some of the neighbours, white as well as black, rallied round, furious at what they saw as an unwarranted intrusion by the Authorities and the Media into an area they understood little about, and cared even less. A petition was organised in support of her right to rebuild the Oracle. The local synagogue and Community Relations Council organised a series of activities to raise money for the new building. And the fight, as they say, still goes on.

The story brings together issues about the shifting geographies of racial conflict, the surrealism of the English sense of home, and the persistence of its attendant insularities within a still racially superior sense of the play of difference in the making of post-colonial Britishness. The 'danger' of Mrs Ntolo's oracle lay not only in its mixing together of sacred and profane, purification and syncretism, but its construction by someone whose own credentials belong to a 'wild' and unassimilable form of hybridity. The point of the story, it seems to me, is not just that it shows how it may still, under certain favourable circumstances, be possible to reconstitute a progressive and popular politics of locality operative across globalised racial divides; it indicates, as well, how a poetics of resistance is continually being recreated; the shifting interface of front lines, backyards continually opens up new cracks in the edifice of modernity and governance. How are we to understand this bizarre attempt to 'support' a 'traditional' structure that does not require it, if not as a futile attempt to prop up an obsolescent model of insularity that might otherwise collapse? The attempt to wrap a vernacular architecture composed from black and Jewish religious influence in the garb of a concrete prefab, to turn it into a kind of Christo-installation in reverse, is doomed to failure. It is not just that this brittle carapace of eurocentrism will crumble away in the face of a structure of much longer duration. It is as if this oracle, by virtue of its very materiality, speaks a metaphysical truth that cannot be expressed in the legal/bureaucratic norms imposed on its existence. This truth is metaphysical because it embodies a principle of hope born of a stubborn, against-all-the-odds, mind-over-matter, 'materialism'. That is the building's scandal, which cannot be erased by any amount of 'reconstruction'. And it points to a poetics of perpetual political beginning, beyond island-story, against which all the bulldozers in the world are powerless.

Aspiration and attitude ... reflections on black Britain in the nineties

Stuart Hall

We need to think about the metaphor of frontlines/backyards and what it might mean in the context of an emergent black British identity. Our instinct is to line up these notions with received ideas of public and private. In the public realm, frontlines are the politicised edge between black culture and white culture; backyards are where some less confrontational, more informal, more complicated, private negotiations might take place. But I don't want to think of them in that way. I want instead to reflect on the mechanisms by which black culture itself – a potential black British identity – comes to be organised around *both* its frontlines and backyards.

We know well enough the pitfalls which open up when we discuss questions to do with black British identity. Inevitably we have to be selective and impressionistic; there are many critical aspects which we are bound to leave out. Most of all, it's difficult to be both positive and critical. One has to accept that, no matter how one tries to lower the temperature of debate, however descriptive one tries to be about the culture which you yourself are inhabiting, there's a great deal invested in it. Consequently innocent description can too easily transmute into an object of desire, and be contested in what might seem unexpected ways. There is no neutral way to discuss what is changing about black British identity.

Even so: it's worth taking the risk of stating that an ethnicity distinctively identifiable as black British is beginning to emerge. By its frontlines here, we don't only mean the politicised frontier lines of confrontation. To me, the term frontlines is a reminder that lines of engagement are always border zones, places where the lines keep moving and changing. Borders are always more porous than they look; everyday when you wake up the frontline has shifted a little. The real question about frontlines is, what is up-front, what is more visible now in the publicly negotiated spaces of difference, around questions of race and black British identities? Backyards are always more difficult to focus conceptually because they are out of sight. They are not policed in the same manner – though they are policed heavily, by communities themselves as well as more obviously by the police! Backlines are especially watched over and regulated by the community. Nevertheless, the familiar and the unfamiliar are allowed to co-exist in backyards to a degree that official frontline spokespersons are wary about recognising.

When I speak about black British identity I'm principally referring to the Afro-Caribbean communities. This may be one of the most important aspects of what I'm trying to say. I have seen perhaps three generations of black British culture since I came to this country in 1951, and I have observed some of the differences from one period to another. There was a very particular moment, politically, in Britain when we would not have made the distinction between Afro-Caribbean and Asian, because, so far as the majority society is concerned, and therefore for us too, the two ethnic groupings were so often treated in exactly the same way that the single term 'black' would suffice. That is no longer the case. To talk about questions of culture is not to recognise a complex, internal cultural segmentation – internal frontlines which cut through and bisect so-called black British identity. Now we are required to be much more specific about where we are drawing these images from and – rather than being able to state unequivocally – we have to invite comments as to the extent to which they apply elsewhere across the different, black communities.

A final caveat. We're talking almost exclusively about younger people. I do not wish in any way to exclude older people from the broader picture. But in this arena of cultural transformation the young generation is bound to constitute a kind of exploratory leading-edge, willing to engage in new cultures which older people, more settled in their ways, don't explore to the same extent. In young people we are likely to see the lineaments of change much more clearly defined.

What follows is a series of perceptions which we offer as so many reflections on a rapidly shifting scene. First we would ask you to think about the deepening internal divisions within and between different black identities, and between the frontlines and the backyards. The curious social fact that we have increasingly to recognise is that of minorities who are doing, relatively speaking, quite well economically, and of majorities who are probably doing worse than they have in a long time. The same ethnic communities are no longer affected by economic and social change in a homogeneous way, but in a way that drives lines of distinction and division between the prospects for those who can imagine something opening up in their own personal trajectories, and for those who still don't see anything at all – a dead-end. This gap is sharper in the United Kingdom – as it is now in the United States – than it has been for a long time. I want to come back to that contradictory reality at the end. However, we need a little bit more uplift before we return to the matter of the backyard.

We now have a situation where black British culture could be described as confident beyond measure in its own identity; that is to say, secure in its difference which, though not absolute in its binary form, is founded on the perception that it will neither retreat nor go away. Though black British culture is rigorously and frequently excluded by some vocal elements in the 'host' society, it does not exclude itself in its own mind. With respect to blackness it is very positively affirmative. However, a corollary which follows is that blackness is no longer necessarily a counter or resistance identity, as it was in the 1970s. The political resonances of black identity have shifted significantly over the last ten or fifteen years. They have moved in the direction of what we may call the 'multicultural' – provided the term is used, not substantively but adjectivally, in the sense of describing the movement toward a genuinely multicultural society. This represents a significant and complex shift: though the term 'multicultural' relates in complicated ways to what is distinctively British, this can only become a reality if 'British' can include the multicultural. There is no longer a prevailing sense that what is British constitutes an ideal to which black culture might want to aspire or assimilate. Thus it is the very meaning and stability of Britishness itself which has been inflected by black culture. It's this *reversal* which signifies a culture confident in its own difference. Black culture in Britain does not now aspire, in what many of us who are older know of as a deep legacy of the colonial relation, caught in Fanon's phrase – 'black skin, white mask' – to mimic or echo Britishness. The people I'm talking about relate to their blackness in terms of an autonomous identity which they do not imagine as tradable in any way.

We can go back to the 1970s, to the high period of Rastafarianism, and to the rediscovery of and re-identification with an 'African' identity – when to be black was constituted by the counter-languages of Black Power, Afro-centrism and reggae. In that period, the notion that black people might exist in Britain who were perfectly comfortable and 'at home' with being black in Britain would have been unthinkable. It might, perhaps, have been part of a longer-term hope or political project; but the fact it would become so *settled* a fact that black people would think of themselves as just going on being black and British ... that was unthinkable. I'm not suggesting everybody now feels comfortably positioned within this emergent new culture of black Britain. The majority of white people don't feel comfortable with it at all. But in cultural or symbolic terms, the 'black presence' today is more palpably and affirmatively *present*, and this does mark an important historic shift.

Being in the world in the 1990s requires, more than hitherto, a styling of the self, a settlement in and with one's own body. At the same time we should recall the extremely contradictory way in which young black people continue, in economic terms, to be at the receiving end of systematic structures of deprivation and marginalisation because of their race. They are doubly disadvantaged in the classical manner, for many do poorly in school, find themselves excluded when young, and then that is doubled up when it comes to employment and opportunities in adult life. And yet in that same moment of exclusion the stylisation of their own racialised bodies is a striking feature of contemporary popular and visual culture, something which has made them *the* defining force in street-oriented British youth culture. Without them, it often seems, white British youth culture simply would not exist.

Street culture is a zone of enforced glamour, and there is nothing more conversant with enforced glamour, enforced sexuality, than the black body. We're talking not only about clothes and fashion and music, but about the culture as a whole. On mainstream television one positively has to search out images which don't manifestly contain a connotation of a sexual kind. In that cultural setting, where the language of a stylised sexuality is ubiquitous, the exotic character of the black body takes on an absolutely powerful charge and becomes a particular and ambivalent subject of desire. There you have the contradiction – of people, many of whom hardly know how they're going to keep body and soul together, who are at the same time the objects of an exotic desire in the youth consumer culture which surrounds them and which gives them an excessive visibility.

We could reflect on another shift. The majority of younger black people we're talking about have come of age in the neo-liberal, post-Thatcher world. The Thatcher epoch was a time which was never wonderfully open and receptive to black people – think of Mrs Thatcher's 'alien wedge' and Norman Tebbit's 'cricket test'. Nevertheless a minority of black people seem to have been able to work their way through the interstices of the enterprise culture. The much-fanfared enterprise culture was certainly not designed for them, but they have a way with a mobile-phone. There *is* a certain symbiosis between the hustling culture and the enterprise culture; every now and again, they almost look like the same thing. So even if you've not been born to or trained in the mysteries of producing yourself as an entrepreneurial subject, you bring to the enterprise culture one or two hustling skills from the margins, and know how to move with them, and it is possible – not to get up to where it counts – but to make a little room in the ante-chambers of power.

This is a minority success-story of a kind – but it is important in the following context. Because there is a black culture now in Britain which allows black people to feel comfortable being black, while fully understanding that most other people are not – that we continue to live in a racist-inscribed world – they are strong on the question of their own rights, and they don't apologise for advancing them. 'This is our due', they seem to say; 'Deliver!' Their grandparents would not have spoken like this. Today it is simply what we mean by *attitude*. This marks a significant political shift. These young people are not reliant on a broader corporate or collectivist culture in order to achieve the recognition of their rights in their own lifetimes. They haven't come out of a collectivist culture which has achieved greater equality and justice for black people, over a period of time, through political struggle. If you look at British culture and ask what have collective and corporate defensive struggles achieved over the years, and what they have delivered for people's everyday lives, you would have to say that, though the long struggle for equal opportunities *has* slowly changed the climate of opinion, the majority of black people have seen the decline of the welfare-state culture, which has been the principal material support of the urban under-privileged to whom they largely belong. And if they had been hanging around waiting for the welfare-state culture to come back and to shore themselves up against hard times, they would have been absolutely nowhere. They had to go out and carve out something for themselves.

This undoubtedly makes black British identity take on a distinctly individualist cast. The period when black politics was the politics of community struggle seems to me profoundly in recession. I don't say this because it's necessarily a virtue, but because descriptively I think it the case. There's a great deal of political consciousness around race at large, but it has increasingly taken the form of people seeing that they've got to carve out something for themselves. If this means that they've got to have a job, and on top of that go to college one or two nights a week, and take a qualification at work, and do something at weekends, have four or five jobs, and run a family and look after their kids, well, that is what life is like, especially for young black women. The reward for these labours is that they won't have a dead-end job forever but might just begin to have a lower-status administrative job, with a modicum of interest and responsibility. Increasingly, black women are taking that route, and not waiting to bring everyone along with them. This version of black British identity has been obliged to find a way through by making something for themselves, through the slog of long, remorseless and difficult work.

One of the lines which distinguishes backyards from frontlines in this respect is the line which I've just noted – the one that runs between black men and black women. If what I've been saying about willingness to push through the interstices is correct, it seems to me unquestionable that black women have on the whole been more successful than men. This is not to moan that because women have advanced, men have been left behind. Far from it. I'm asking you to think about why it might be that in this particular kind of free-enterprise, hustling world of the 1980s and 1990s, black women on the whole are better at it than black men – and whether this has anything to do with the different styles of resistance to racism and their different modes, especially in school and youth cultures.

This is a deeply *aspirant* culture. Maybe this is a dirty word for many people, but not for the people who aspire. We are talking about young people who think they can do things, who are convinced about their capacity to do more than their society offers, to take on more responsibility, to go further, to learn more, to be promoted, to perform, and who know that the chances of being given the opportunities to do so are slim. But they continue to aspire – not to fill positions because they are 'white', since they are perfectly happy with the possibility that they can be successful *and* black, if only society would allow it. The way we think of race as structuring avenues of relative aspiration and achievement are shifting rapidly in comparison with two decades ago.

Stuart Hall speaking at the Frontlines / Backyards conference.

I don't want to say very much about the uneven and selective character of this visibility. I'm perfectly aware that if you look at the mass media you notice a very profound difference in where you find black faces and where you don't, in what kinds of stories and about what sorts of experiences. Even so, perhaps we don't recognise sufficiently the degree to which in certain areas of public visibility black faces are becoming *de rigueur*. Take sport in Britain. Nothing is closer to the heart of the average Englishman – as opposed to the fields where classically blacks have been outstanding, such as cricket or boxing – than the heartland of soccer. There isn't an occasion when you can pick up a decent Sunday paper, with its photos of Saturday's matches, and not see black faces. Are blacks in the boardrooms of the clubs? Of course not. Are they relatively powerless in the institutions which organise the game? Of course. The question is whether they have any currency, any visibility in the culture of sport where the nation's myths and meanings are fabricated. The answer must be 'yes', and to say this is to note the significant degree to which the culture has turned in the past fifteen or so years.

There isn't space to go into questions of music in detail, but the leading role of rap, jungle and drum-and-base, not only in itself, as an expressive moment in black British urban culture, but as an arena of crossover, of desire, as part of the culture of working-class and middle-class white wannabees – this is instructive. Here, without question, the leading edge, symbolically, in terms of what goes next, the inner stylistic transformations that keep the music moving, is defined by young black people. We're not talking here about taking over, but about the shifts of terrain which allow a new set of relations to arise, in which young black people can possess their blackness in a society still ugly with the inscriptions of racism. This is a culture which signals a new axis along which the structures of racial difference move, and which anticipates the possibilities for a genuinely multicultural Britain – a transformation requiring the remaking of white Britain too.

At one stage the images that might have governed that relationship to blackness would have been underwritten by an African signature, an African-centred, Afro-centric inflexion. This doesn't have much to do with the question whether, in the 1960s, Afro-Caribbean people knew much about Africa – they didn't. It had to do with the fact that to *connote* Africa was a way of locating one's identity in an alternative source of authenticity, in 'roots', and in a power which was not white. Similarly, in the 1960s and the 1970s, to connote the Caribbean – which was the latent source of the images of the reggae revolution – was a way of doing the same. It marked the difference from Europe. What strikes one now most pervasively and paradoxically about black British identity is the degree to which it has been Americanised. Its imagery, its stylistic dynamics, are very powerfully drawn from black America. That is not to deny that it has been indigenised in a particularly British mode – creating a genuinely new syncretic culture – or that all leads from America. But if you ask what is the ideal image which seems to have structured the field of black popular culture in the 1980s, it tends to come back again and again to a kind of black Americanisation. This is a profound shift, behind which lies a shift in the relationship of the Caribbean itself to the United States. Present here too are the reverberations from particular family histories, drawing from the experiences of those black British families who have re-emigrated to the United States. The lines of communication and confluence that have thus opened up between black British culture and black American culture are very rich, intense and complex.

Despite the fact that few commentators on the black cultural scene would agree with many of the descriptive images I have offered, and even fewer would view them positively, I suspect that almost everyone *would* be able to attach some images to the trends I've been describing. We need other voices to describe what is going on. We talk about cultural identities as if they have no specificity or content. Yet often we don't have a clue what a black British identity would actually look like. Most people have no idea how much would have to be displaced, in the traditional conceptions of Englishness or Britishness, for people to feel that this was an inhabitable identity, even if it came wrapped in lingering forms of racism.

I want to end not by reminding you again that we are talking about a frontline – an area of high visibility, of a leading-edge *minority* success version of a black British identity. One would have to put, right next door to that minority story, the extensive evidence one has of the persistence of more exclusive and excluded black worlds – backyards – where the signifiers remain, not open but closed, where black culture remains boxed-in, oppressed, subject to organised racism, defensive, enclosed within a limited territorial space. One would need to talk about the importance, the value that is given in these more closed, exclusive black worlds to *attitude*, which has a kind of currency in different versions in both frontlines and backyards, which has an expressive life in music, in dancing, in the rituals and exoticisms of the black body, and which has profound consequences indeed for how black masculinity and femininity are being lived and experienced.

There are some positive aspects to the persistence of this more enclosed black backyard culture – the world of 'the posse', real and imaginary. Most young people these days belong to imaginary posses; but a few do belong to real ones. One of the most important values placed on them is their capacity to look after themselves. 'The posse' is a self-enclosing, self-sustaining, quasi-autonomous world where everybody has to look after themselves, because nobody will look after you. It has its own territorial delimitation, its own codes in dress and music and so on, which are part of the attempt to constitute itself as a self-sufficient cultural world. It is important to set this backyard experience alongside the dilemmas of a more negotiating, success-orientated, aspirational, out-going frontline cultural politics, which is the minority experience I have tried to evoke here.

As a consequence of three or four decades of intense black migration, specifically from the Caribbean, into British society, we have been passing through at least three, maybe more, differentiated ethnic-identity moments. We have seen, from the 1980s and the 1990s, the emergence of a very distinctive, different, minority cultural formation, whose future we know little about, whose sociological composition is still very amorphous and ambivalent. This new frontline black culture is not, in any clear-cut sense, defined by socio-economic criteria; it doesn't derive in any straightforward way from the distribution of material opportunities and resources within the black community, or between the black and white communities. It isn't a class phenomenon in the sense in which the structuring of disadvantage by the labour market in the 1950s and the 1960s clearly demarcated the black community's socio-economic position and identification. It is, in a complicated way, engaged with the redefinition, from the inside, of what it is to be black and British at the end of the twentieth century. It does have profound implications for Britain's mainstream negotiation of itself, in relation to its own imperial past, in relation to Europe, and to its place in a wider, competitive, global system. The black community in general has, at the moment, no large-scale view of that wider process. It is not itself mobilised for or engaged in a debate about what a more multicultural British society ought to be in relation, for example, to the Third World or Europe. Nevertheless, it is at the centre, the pivot, of that historic renegotiation.

And – just to close with the most depressing feature of all – I would like to say that what I've been talking about does not seem to have much resonance in new Labour. It is not clear that Blair's advisers would know what or who we have been talking about. Its future does not give any indication of shaping new Labour's calculations about the making of a 'New Britain'. It is a blanked-out space as far as the language of New Labour is concerned, written out of the imagined post-Millennium New Britain which the government is struggling to construct.

'I BELONG TO WHOEVER WANTS ME'

Mary Chamberlain

'I had no nation now but the imagination'
(Derek Walcott, *The Schooner Flight*)

Charles

> I see myself in many disguises ... like UK Black ... European ... I'm lost here. I'm looking for the word ... that fits the description. Can I be Anglo-Caribbean?[1]

Peter

> I belong to whoever wants me ... if British people don't want me, what's the point of making yourself part of something that doesn't want you? And if the Bajans don't want me, then why make yourself ... Bajan, when they don't want you either? If the Chinese want me ... I'll be Chinese. *I'm who wants me ...*[2]

Shola

> When I go back to the West Indies, even my accent changes, or something about my voice ... people ask me there if I'm from certain parts. Like, in Jamaica, they'll ask me if I'm from East Kingston. In Barbados, they'll ask me if I'm from a certain part of Barbados. Either it's because I pick up the local dialect or something, and you can be just at home in all of these things. I'm not confused about my identity ... *I'm equally at home anywhere.*[3]

Between 1948 and 1973 approximately 550,000 people of Caribbean birth came to Britain, the majority arriving before the 1962 Immigration Act effectively cut off further immigration. The early debate on Caribbean immigration to Britain was located within a framework of race relations which assumed economic necessity as the engine of migration, permanency in settlement, and placed integration and assimilation as both the goal and yardstick of migrant success, reflected in various contemporary studies.[4]

The migration from the Caribbean was subsequently supplemented by that from the Indian subcontinent and by the 1970s it was no longer possible to equate all migration with that from the Caribbean. Integration as a goal was replaced by 'multi-culturalism', defined in 1968 by the then Home Secretary Roy (now Lord) Jenkins who argued that assimilation was neither possible nor desirable and that, instead, Britain should recognise 'cultural diversity' and encourage 'mutual tolerance'. The shift became reflected in the literature as scholars such as Rex, Cross and Peach teased out the historical, social and cultural factors specific to immigrant behaviour and response in the host society.[5]

1. BB23/1/2/1/57.

2. BB78/1/1/B/45.

3. BB80/1/1/2/51.

4. Joyce Egginton, *They Seek a Living*, Hutchinson, London 1957; Ruth Glass, *London's Newcomers*, Harvard University Press, Cambridge, Massachusetts 1961; Sheila Patterson, *Dark Strangers*, Penguin, London 1964; R.B. Davison, *Black British*, London Institute of Race Relations, Oxford University Press 1966. See also R.B. Davison, *West Indian Migrants*, Oxford University Press, London 1962; Ceri Peach, *West Indian Migration to Britain: a social geography*, Oxford University Press, London 1968; Dilip Hero, *Black British White British: a history of race relations in Britain*, Penguin, London 1973; Nancy Foner, *Jamaican Farewell: Jamaican migrants in London*, Routledge and Kegan Paul, London 1979.

5. John Rex and Sally Tomlinson, *Colonial Immigrants in a British City*, Routledge and Kegan Paul, London 1979; John Rex, 'The heritage of slavery and social disadvantage', in Colin Brock (ed), *The Caribbean in Europe*, Frank Cass, London 1986; Malcolm Cross, 'Migration and exclusion: Caribbean echoes and British realities' in Colin Brock, *op.cit.*;

Malcolm Cross and
Han Entzinger (eds),
*Lost Illusions:
Caribbean minorities
in Britain and the
Netherlands,*
Routledge, London
1988; Ceri Peach,
'Patterns of Afro-
Caribbean migration
and settlement in
Britain, 1945-1981'
in Colin Brock,
op.cit.

6. Harry
Goulbourne,
*Ethnicity and
Nationalism in Post-
Imperial Britain,*
Cambridge
University Press,
Cambridge 1991.
See, for instance,
Catherine Hall,
'White visions, black
lives: the free
villages of Jamaica',
*History Workshop
Journal 36,* 1993.
Stuart Hall,
'Cultural identity
and diaspora' in
J.Rutherford (ed)
*Identity: community,
culture and differ-
ence,* Lawrence &
Wishart, London
1990; 'The local and
the global: globalisa-
tion and ethnicity' in
A.D. King (ed),
*Culture,
Globalisation and
the World System:
contemporary condi-
tions for the repre-
sentations of
identity,* Macmillan,
Basingstoke 1991;
Paul Gilroy, *The
Black Atlantic:
modernity and
double consciousness,*
Verso, London 1993.

7. Figures calculated
from Caribbean
census and OPCS
census data.

8. UK census
returns 1971, 1981,
1991, OPCS. Figures
computed from UK
census returns 1981-

Recent studies have distanced themselves from the race relations/multi-cultural 'paradigm' and have turned the focus onto re-thinking notions of ethnicity, nationalism and identity. Contemporary and historical studies such as those by Harry Goulbourne and Catherine Hall investigate the interaction between the political and historical meanings of British and colonial/migrant identities, while scholars such as Stuart Hall, Paul Gilroy and Homi Bhabha move beyond the location of ethnicity, and leap the borders of the nation-state, into a construction of identity which stresses culture, mobility, hybridity and relationality, moving the debate in the process from migration to diaspora.[6]

We can, however, look at this from another perspective. The Caribbean community in Britain represents less than one per cent of the population of Britain, but the number of migrants as a percentage of the population of the *home* countries is sometimes large. Between 1951 and 1971, 7 per cent of the population of Jamaica, for instance, migrated to Britain, and 12 per cent of the population of Barbados.[7] These figures suggest very different cultural and economic pressures operated in each of the islands to encourage migration. Equally, there has been a significant but differential reduction in the size of the Caribbean communities in the last decade, some of it as the result of death, but mostly due to re- and return migration. Between the census points 1971 and 1991, the Barbadian and Jamaican communities have declined by 17 per cent (from 27,055 to 22,294, and 171,775 to 142,483 respectively) and the indications are that they continue to decline.[8]

Such differences in the patterns of migration, settlement and return require explanation. At the same time, the Caribbean migrants who arrived in Britain during the 1950s and 1960s are now comfortably into middle age. Many of their children were born and brought up in Britain. Many are now grandparents. There has been a qualitative change in the structure of the Caribbean community in Britain. At one level it is a stable community with established lineages and networks; at another, it clearly retains elements of transnational mobility. Both features require fresh investigation and raise the question of the extent to which the Caribbean communities in Britain retain or adapt features of their distinctive cultures and traditions.

The Caribbean has always been a hybrid, syncretic culture. There is also a culture and tradition of migration which engages historically with other social and cultural goals, including the 'open' goal of migration *per se.* Recent Caribbean-based studies of migration such as those by Bonham Richardson, Elizabeth Thomas-Hope and Karen Fog Olwig have refocused on questions of causation by pointing to the links between individual choice and the specificity of environment, culture and migration, highlighting what Thomas-Hope terms the 'homeward orientation', or what Palmer chronicles as the 'circularity' of Caribbean migration, emphasising the internationalisation of those Caribbean families through the extension of the domestic unit abroad, and placing migration within a continuing historical perspective.[9]

Equally, research such as that by Philip Kasinitz, Constance Sutton and Ransford Palmer in the United States, where migration from the Caribbean has been a feature for over a century, suggests that these migrants retain a Caribbean identity across generations and remain centred within kinship networks which link the Caribbean and North America.[10] It is my contention not only that the Caribbean community in Britain now displays elements which parallel those of North America, but that these elements are neither random nor coincidental. Rather, they contain elements common to a Caribbean *migratory* culture which not only functions as an explanatory factor in migration itself, but continues to function as a cohesive and distinctive force within the host society. It may be transformed across generations and modified by local conditions, but not eradicated by them.

This research, based on eighty-five life-story interviews across three generations of twenty Barbadian families, explores the extent to which a migration ideology continues to shape the perspectives, behaviour and identities of Caribbean migrants, their children and grandchildren, who occupy serial positions of identity and consciousness, moulded in the Caribbean and modulated across the generations and across the seas. The story of Caribbean migration is an international one, a syncretic one, and a continuing one.

It is this story which I wish to emphasise. Migration has been central to the social and cultural formations of Barbados certainly from 1838 and arguably for considerably longer. There has scarcely been a generation of Barbadian families who has not been touched, and shaped, by migration and its absences, at a literal, metaphysical, cultural and historical level. For those who came to Britain in the 1950s and 1960s, the duration of their stay proved longer than anticipated. However frequent the letters and the visits home, the family became characterized by geographical and generational distancing, and by an isolation from the wider networks of kinship in Barbados. The children of migrants in Britain experienced a mirror image of the absence of close kin which characterized *their* parents' childhood in Barbados. This absence, of family and home, has been an integral component of the dynamic of diaspora, moulding the narratives and subjectivities of the migrants and their children, creating what George Lamming describes as 'the consolation of freedom'.[11] Families themselves foster notions of roots and exile as points of reference, explanation and survival in the host societies. For the first migrants to Britain, 'home' was the physical space in which they found their primary identity and Barbados became for most the site of unambiguous allegiance, heightened by a resistance to be incorporated in Britain under a homogenous black ethnicity in which their old rivals, the Jamaicans, had hegemony.[12] Clearly, for this generation raised in Barbados, the cultural roots and family

1991, OCPS.

9. Elizabeth Thomas-Hope, *Explanation in Caribbean Migration*, Warwick University Caribbean Studies Series, Macmillan, London 1993; Elizabeth Thomas-Hope, 'Caribbean diaspora, the inheritance of slavery: migration from the Commonwealth Caribbean' in Colin Brook (ed) *op.cit.*; Karen Fog Olwig, 'The migration experience: Nevisian women at home and abroad' in Janet Momsen (ed), *Women and Change in the Caribbean*, Ian Randle, Kingston 1993; Ransford Palmer, *op.cit.*; Karen Fog Olwig, *op.cit.*

10. Philip Kasinitz, *Caribbean New York: Black immigrants and the politics of race*, Cornell University Press, Ithaca, New York 1992; Constance Sutton and Elsa Chaney (eds), *Caribbean Life in New York: sociocultural dimensions*, Centre for Migration Studies of New York, New York City 1994; Ransford Palmer, 'Caribbean development and the migration imperative' in Ransford Palmer (ed), *In Search of a Better Life: perspectives on migration from the Caribbean*, Praeger, New York 1990.

11. George Lamming, *In the Castle of My Skin*, Macmillan, London 1987.

12. This resistance to, and differentiation from, Jamaica was exploited by the Barbados Liaison Officer in his negotiations with prospective British employers, who emphasised the long-standing reputation of Barbadians as hard-working, law-abiding and loyal colonials.

models had a direct, primary, influence, establishing defined attitudes towards migration, its anticipated goals and patterns of survival. For them, their grandparents, other old 'ancestants', the proximity of an extended family, the village streets and family plots, had shaped their memories. But for their children born in Britain, those memories were not only one-remove, but foreign. Family continuities, which made sense of, and for, their parents have had to be reconstructed by their children within a context of mobility and movement not of their choosing and devoid of their parents' rationale. For this generation, there is also another meaning to absence. The early generation of migrants, brought up (and migrating) under colonialism, considered themselves 'British', but its meaning for them cohabited with an alternative cultural and national allegiance. Barbados was a nation and, after 1966, a politically autonomous one. Choice was a possibility. Many of the British-born Barbadians express a sense of exclusion from Barbados citing, with irony, their 'Englishness' as its cause. They also feel a more articulate sense of dislocation and displacement in Britain, of belonging to neither one side nor the other.

As the generation of British-born black Barbadians have children themselves, and as they experience their parents' return to Barbados, the family models are extending and, paradoxically, the links with Barbados are becoming closer. They move out of the role of cultural broker, which characterized their childhood, and into that of cultural transmitter, finding their 'consolation of freedom' within the traditions of the family and its values. Subjectivity and identity, like memory, are never static and are always in a process of creation and transformation. Now, they run parallel with the changes in the shape and function of the family.

Let me start with David.

> How do I identify myself? ... at school, you was black, ... When it comes to cricket, 'Oh go on, West Indies! Give England a thrashing!' If England are playing a football match ... and if there's four or five black guys, 'Go on England!' How can I identify myself? Realistically I'm British, black British ... I'm trying to look for a final word to say what I am. I'm black, that's a fact. I suppose British West Indian. I don't know how you sort it out.[13]

13. BB77/1/1/B/35-36.

David was born in South London in 1966. Within one statement, he moves between black British and British West Indian. David's dilemma is not unusual; most migrant children, of whatever ethnic origin, stay bound to the cultural reins of their parents and juggle with ambiguous and sometimes contradictory allegiances. What is relevant is how and why allegiances differ, to what extent and with what effect.

The culture of Barbadian migration is permeated with the expectation of return. Within that culture family structures have, and can, adapt to the demands of migration.[14] All of those we interviewed anticipated that their initial stay in Britain would be between three and five years. Many, indeed, planned on that basis, leaving children in Barbados in the care of relatives and tolerating, as a temporary expedient, racism and poor social conditions. Children born or brought up in Britain lived with the potential not only of their parents' return migration but also, by extension, their own migration. To this end, many parents consciously transferred a notion of Barbados to their British-born children, reinforcing it with visits 'home' and maintaining close ties with relatives there. In some instances, young children were returned 'home' to be reared by grandparents or other kin. Children were aware of a restlessness, a sense that 'home' was absent in this country, located elsewhere. The intensity of this culturation was, however, closely related to the feasibility of return.

David's mother Beryl migrated to Britain in 1961, intending to stay for five years. Migration had shaped Beryl's childhood. Her grandfather had migrated to Panama, her uncle to Cuba and her father to Trinidad. Beryl, like her mother and grandmother, was brought up without a father but with the help and support of the extended family. Her great-grandfather's migration and return had provided the family with land which helped sustain successive generations; but her father's migration, about which she felt 'angry' had left her with an emotional and material loss. Improvement, and absence, the goal and the reality of migration, were forceful family models for Beryl and a formative influence on her attitudes towards bringing up her own children in Britain.

Unlike many other women in the sample, Beryl did not work outside the home while her children were young, nor did she consider sending her children home to her mother in Barbados. They lived on her husband's wages as a Post Office driver. Unable to save, much less buy property, they were locked into a cycle of deferment, with the prospect of 'home' receding into the distance and the 'promise' of England crumbling like pie crust. Beryl felt displaced in, and entrapped by, England. With return no longer viable, neither Beryl nor her husband – as David recalled – spoke directly about Barbados though it encroached as a stern metaphysical presence. He considered his parents to be the 'strictest' in the neighbourhood. They emphasized education, and restricted when, where and with whom he could play.

When David was eight the family visited Barbados where he met his grandparents and other family members for the first time. He was, however, shocked by the living conditions and the children who taunted him, calling him 'English potato'. The visit evoked a mixed response, of familial acceptance and public displacement. Nevertheless, it enabled flesh to be put on his parents memories, as Barbados also entered into his own. He left 'loving Barbados' and with a new curiosity about his parents' relationship to the island.

The visit, and his maturing years, resulted in a growing awareness of his

14. See Christine Barrow, 'Finding the Support: strategies for survival, in *Social and Economic Studies* (Jamaica) June 1986; Isa Maria Soto, 'West Indian child fostering: Its role in migrant exchange' in Constance Sutton and Elsa Chaney, *Caribbean Life in New York City: sociocultural dimensions*, New York, Center for Migration Studies of New York, Center for Migration Studies of New York Inc, 1994.

parents' background and his own immediate environment. Prior to the visit to Barbados, David and his siblings identified primarily with the children in their London neighbourhood, among whom his parents' attitudes, behaviour and ethnicity flagged a difference which they neither liked nor understood. Ironically, it was that childhood visit to Barbados which put this primary identity in profile. In their neighbourhood in London there were a number of Bajan friends and relatives who, for Beryl and her husband, had offered a continuity with 'home', contacts and support. For David, these people now became a source of culture and heritage and, ultimately, a model. At the same time, and by contrast, David was growing up in the world of the working-class inner city, where he became increasingly aware of his *own* ethnicity. As a keen football player and fan, he experienced discrimination and racial taunts, an experience replicated at school and in the apprenticeship system.

David is assertive of his own ethnicity, which is now given another dimension as he identifies his cultural values with his parents and the Barbadian community. David has a young daughter and lives mostly with his girlfriend. He is not married. But then, neither were his maternal grandparents in Barbados, nor were his own parents until after the birth of their children. His family arrangements conform to many of the traditional patterns of marriage and family prevalent in Barbados, where grandmothers have a role in the care and upbringing of children. Young children in Barbados have privileged access to their grandparents' generation, a feature which David missed out on in Beryl's decision not to return her children to their grandmother's care in Barbados. David's own daughter is, however, cared for most of the week by his mother. Ironically, David's household and family arrangements, as with others in this sample and elsewhere, are conforming increasingly to the Caribbean rather than the British 'norm' of family structure. A lengthy stay in Britain has not weakened traditional family forms. On the contrary, as the generations extend, this duration has enabled these family forms to be reconstructed and, with this reconstruction, a strengthening of the cultural ties with Barbados and a positive espousal of Barbadian culture have come about.

Beryl and her husband, however, are now planning to go 'home'. Although their return will create a 'void' for David, it will also establish direct links for him and his daughter with Barbados. It is this prospect which is forcing him to rethink his own sense of self. He is black British; he is also British West Indian. The impending social and emotional disruption to David's family life, at the point where it was beginning to replicate Barbadian custom, has forced him to reappraise his own position.

This reappraisal is partly the function of maturity and awareness; but it is also related to the shifting life cycle of his family of origin and creation. His parents' absence will strengthen David's links with Barbados and become a part of his daughter's cultural inheritance.

As ties with the Caribbean are re-learned across generations, and as the family structures continue to provide links and continuities, other aspects of migrant Caribbean culture in Britain are evolving. For instance, David's aim is to own his own business. All the Barbadians in this sample wished their children to take full advantage of the opportunities afforded in Britain, a not unusual goal given the genesis of Barbadian migration. David's ambitions clearly conform to this ethos of self-improvement. At the same time, he argues:

> if you're white ... there's always someone ... a dad, who always (or) he's got a mate, he's getting a job in his law office, or his engineering firm, 'get your boy over, we'll teach him a bit about heating, we'll find room for him.' That's the advantage they've got at the moment, and what black kids haven't got.[15]

15. BB771/1/B/41.

For his parents and their generation, the Barbadian migrant networks established in Britain were essential for survival. Migrants entered into the 'grapevine' before they left Barbados and became fully fledged members of it on arrival. It was through the grapevine that accommodation and employment were found. The grapevine reproduced village structures left behind (indeed, were often comprised of kin and former neighbours) and sustained the values of support and sharing which had been part of the social fabric of Barbados. David's ambition to own a business is located not so much in the profit ethos as in the desire to reproduce on a more permanent basis the migrant networks of his parents' generation and to provide support for his and others' children. Black people, he argues, need their own structures and infrastructures in order to succeed.

David's views are also echoed by Peter, who was born in Reading in 1967 and is the father of two young children. He is now separated from his girlfriend, their mother, but shared the childcare with her and his own mother. Like David, his own sense of allegiance is mobile: 'I belong to whoever wants me'.

Peter's parents migrated to England as children, to join their respective parents who had already settled there. Peter's maternal grandmother, Estelle, was born in 1930 but raised by her maternal grandmother, a plantation labourer. In 1950 Estelle gave birth to Peter's mother, Beulah. When Estelle migrated to Britain in 1956, she left Beulah in the care of this grandmother. Beulah's great uncle had migrated to Cuba in 1920 and the family never saw him again. A sense of loss permeated her childhood – of this uncle, her mother, and her father and was reinforced when she joined her mother in England, losing her adored grandmother. Her family loyalties remained firmly attached to her great-grandmother in Barbados, and were strengthened by her relationship with her own father, whose own sense of self, family and black identity was a source of guidance, comfort and inspiration.

Nevertheless, the extent of her anglicisation was brought home to her when, after twenty years, she returned to Barbados for a visit. She was thirty years old.

> I'll never forget this feeling ... do you know what really got me? The men ... I'm seeing these men. They're tall. Black men in England aren't tall, they're not erect, they're always working as if they've got a burden ... these men look(ed) so proud ... those are the things, as a black woman, born in the Caribbean ... (that) took on a new meaning for me ... black men, black professionals, just a sense of pride that I think the black man in Britain has lost as a result of living in a culture that is ... alien and hostile and I didn't realise until I went back, that we had changed, and we've adapted to accommodate living here ... if you're proud in England, and you're black, you're seen as uppity, or having a chip on your shoulder.[16]

16. BB451/2/1/46.

She made up her mind then to return to Barbados and, as Peter recalls, to impart to her children 'the love of the island'.

As a result, he says, 'I always knew where I came from'. Returning as a child to Barbados for visits was he says, 'like, for me, going home'. Peter's grandparents were the generation who had migrated in the 1950s and as a result he was surrounded by uncles, aunts and cousins from both sides who gathered together once or twice a week. He stayed regularly with his maternal grandmother who helped look after him while his mother worked. Family life in Britain retained many of the traditional features of Barbados, and Barbados, at first hand and at one remove, was a prominent feature of his childhood reinforced by his parents' – and in particular his mother's – determination to return, to which end they both worked, saved and invested. Barbados, and its absence, for Beulah and her husband assumed a metaphorical importance, and entered centrally into Peter's cultural heritage and imagination. 'Home' had a physical presence beyond Britain. In the meantime, Barbadian culture was retained in the shape and fabric of his family life, and was replicated and reinforced by the Barbadian community in Reading.

In many other ways, his experience of schooling, his apprenticeship (as a professional footballer) and his own experience in business (he is a car trader) were comparable to David's. Like David, he feels he needs to recreate a black network for the next generation to inherit.

Peter's parents have now both returned to Barbados. Peter's maternal grandparents (who were not married, and have separate households and families) have also returned to the island. Yet despite his love for Barbados, and the positive role which Bajan culture played in his life, Peter does not wish to return there. He is uncertain how he could make a living and, more particularly, feels displaced there. By the same token, he is not committed to England and would consider re-migrating to Canada, as did his grandmother before her return to Barbados. England, for the time being, is where he will stay, and carve out an autonomous existence. Yet he has returned, with his children, for visits in recent years and it is their Barbadian heritage which he wishes to instill in them:

> ... if I don't tell my kids about Granny A and Grandad B and about my Mum ... and cook them rice and peas and chicken and West Indian dishes, then they're not going to know anything else ... that's why people like the Jews are so strong because that's been in every generation, they remember the Holocaust, they remember the Bible, and that's been put through them, and that goes on and goes on ... and we forget. If you ask kids now about slavery, they couldn't even tell you about slavery, or when it was abolished or whatever ... you know, problems we had to go through, because they're not interested. All they're interested about is money. There's no values, they ain't got no values.[17]

17. BB78.1/1/30-31.

Consequently, he is conscious of bringing up his children 'exactly the same way' as his parents reared him. Above all, however, he wishes to provide them with a firm identity.

> I'm very passionate about my people and I don't think why I shouldn't be ... when a black person is speaking passionately about his colour, and something he loves, then you start being called a racist. But what am I supposed to do? ... For too many years we've lived bad, and lived like dogs, and been the servants and been the workers ... It's no good one of us living good and ten living bad, we've all got to come together and make it better. And until we realise that, and know where we're going, then we're not going to end up with anything ...[18]

18. BB78.1/1/2/49.

However clear his identity, his allegiances remain migratory. His 'consolation of freedom' he finds in a continuing diaspora, the seeds of future wanderings. He feels displaced in Britain and in Barbados, although he passionately espouses its cultural values, which his parents refused to compromise, and locates his own ethnicity within them. He will, moreover, bring up his children to hold those values and retain their links with his parents in Barbados, thus continuing the contacts between Barbados and Britain, and the structures of the 'transnational' family which have been a consistent historic feature of Caribbean migration, supporting both the migrant and his/her family and accounting for the maintenance and resilience of an autonomous Caribbean culture in the host societies.

Finally Shola, who was born in Leeds in 1969 and plans 'to go home to the Caribbean eventually, but not until we've got a lot behind us, which we can't do just yet ... it's a case of making the best use of the years that coming up now, from experiences that I've had, and my parents have had, and not to make the same mistakes they've made.'[19]

19. BB80/1/1/B/48.

Shola is the eldest of Jeffrey's six children. Her mother was born in

Jamaica. Shola sees herself as 'everything' – British, Barbadian, Jamaican and, by adoption, Kittician but, as she says, 'I'm not confused about my identity ... I'm equally at home anywhere.'[20]

20. BB80/1/1/2/51.

Mobile allegiances appear to be a common thread which runs through all the young people's narratives, running parallel with a positive black identity. For Shola, and like other young women in the sample, her black identity was articulated as emerging alongside an awareness of gender, as she began not only to experience, but to interpret and categorize the racism and sexism she experienced. She refused to be categorised as, as she put it, 'a happy, laughing, smiling nigger ... I can't be like that ... they don't want you to kick out ... against the system, or to break out of the mould that they've got you in.'[21]

21. BB80/1/1/2/34-35.

It is a position which, by her own admission, makes for few friends. She 'switches off' at work and in public spaces, but at home ensures 'I've got people that I want around me ... I feel safe ... with the surroundings, with what I've made them ... who I choose to be with and who I choose to exclude.'[22]

22. BB80/1/2/1/55.

Racism, and her response to it, autonomy, has been placed by her in a generational context, the most appropriate rationale to contextualise her experiences. Racism in Britain she argues is 'ingrained' and:

> will become subtler. I mean, it's very subtle now ... and we're being told that we've got a chip on our shoulder. But the fact is that we're carrying the anger and the experience of our parents and our grandparents and our great-grandparents, and our great-great-grandmothers who have been abused by slave-masters and anger is then passed down through generations ... and to see it happening today, but in different forms, it's very difficult to live with that ... If you don't fit into a particular mould, you're seen as a trouble maker. Now ... I've chosen areas of my life to pursue and things to pull away from.[23]

23. BB801/2/1/56-57.

Shola trained as a radiographer. Children and marriage are on the back burner. Her primary focus is to travel, to earn money and, at the end of the day, to go to the Caribbean to live. England is an expedience towards her future elsewhere, rather than being a future in itself. Shola's ambitions are particularly migratory, or diasporic, and her identity as well as allegiances the most clearly worked out, for which:

> I thank God for parents who have, at least, shown me ... a path, or a way to take, rather than just being left to go any old how, and with no identity ... no family support.[24]

24. Ibid.

But what of her parents? Her mother, from Jamaica, is planning to re-migrate to the United States. Her father, Jeffrey, came to Britain from Barbados in 1962 planning to stay for five years before travelling on. His plans mirrored those of his father, Garfield, who travelled with much the same ambitions, like Garfield's mother before him. Neither Garfield nor Jeffrey fulfilled their ambitions. Garfield lives in Barbados with his remaining daughter, on the remittances returned from his other children who migrated to North America. According to Garfield, Jeffrey never sends money. According to Jeffrey, he sent money home to Barbados every two weeks when he first arrived, but, 'He don't think ... I've got to pay for a mortgage ... I'm not in a room, I'm not on my own ... (emphasis added)'[25]

25. BB2/1/2/1/66.

Although Jeffrey was a skilled worker, he did not always find regular employment. As a result, he travelled around England and Europe in search of work. He would return to Barbados 'tomorrow', he says, 'and build a ... nice house ... but I'm not in a position.' It is not only the lack of funds which prevents his return. It is also loss of face.

Jeffrey argues that his father 'done well' and accounts for this success by the fact that his father 'was on his own.' Garfield also believes that Jeffrey 'done well', and his failure to return to Barbados or help out is the result either of parsimony or profligacy. The mythology of migration – of journey and reward – has become the means by which they have interpreted and made sense of each other's lives. It was these implicit statements of unrealised dreams which Shola inherited.

For her father, as for her grandfather, the reward of migration was located firmly back in Barbados, to return as rich men and build a 'nice house'. This is the ethos which Shola, though born in Britain, inherited. Shola's comment, that 'one thing England is good for, is to make money' is not innocent; it contains within it the ambitions and rationale of at least two migrant generations. She intends to succeed where her father and grandfather failed. No missed opportunities, or distant dreams. She has learnt from her parents' mistakes.

For Shola is 'on her own.' She has no children to support, and no remittances to return. Her earnings are her own. She took full advantage of the educational and economic opportunities offered. With a professional training, she can be relatively assured of a regular income. As a confident and assured young black woman she is, as she says, 'at home anywhere', free to make her own professional and domestic choices. Unlike her father she is not entrapped by, nor peripheral to, a hostile economy. Jeffrey's complaint, that he is 'not on his own' is also not culturally innocent. Caribbean living arrangements permit a wide range of individual choice for men and women, reflecting and reproducing not only a strong sense of individualism, but highly adaptive family structures which have, among other things, enabled and supported migration. Jeffrey considers himself weighed down by his domestic responsibilities. Such responsibilities, for his father when he migrated to the United States, were shared by the wider family in the Caribbean, by his wife, her mother, by Jeffrey. This enabled Garfield to pursue his migrant career alone, but such support was denied to Jeffrey in

England. Shola is not a pioneer migrant. At present she has a family in England. But as she says, she 'has chosen' and the path she has chosen reflects the independence and responsibility characteristic of many Caribbean women. Already she has land in the Caribbean and has a stake in that culture which is certain to be passed on to her children:

> I will show them. I will tell them. I've been shown and told things, but I will tell them more, so they can avoid the mistakes that my parents have made, and mistakes that I have made. And hopefully be more aware ... of this racism that will eat away at them.[26]

26. BB80/1/2/1/57.

In the early literature of Caribbean migration to Britain, emphasis was placed on the need to integrate and assimilate. This literature disregarded the culture of migration which had always precluded such assimilationist trends in favour of eventual return. To this end, parents imparted to their children a sense of Barbados and maintained the family structures across the ocean. As already indicated, some British-born children were sent back to Barbados or, like Beulah, left in Barbados until of an age when they could join their parents in Britain. Clearly, for those children, the links with Barbados are particularly strong, but for all children the prospect and reality of their parents' return has strengthened the cultural and emotional links with the island. The children, and increasingly the grandchildren, now play a critical role in fostering and maintaining those links. Paradoxically, the Barbadian community is becoming more, not less, creolised over time. Moreover, as the generations mature, the continuities in traditional family structure among the generation of Barbadians born or raised in Britain, suggest that the family itself may have become a statement of cultural and ethnic identity, as well as a vital mechanism in the strategy of survival. It will also offer a network of support for migrant families which will reinforce the cultural values of the family, and for the individuals within it, as well as providing – as they have done historically in the Caribbean – a trusted strategy for survival.

This article is based on 'Absence and the "Consolation of Freedom"' from Mary Chamberlain Narratives of Exile and Return, Warwick University Caribbean Studies, Macmillan 1997. I am grateful to the Nuffield Foundation whose grant enabled me to conduct this research. Pseudonyms have been used throughout.

INSIDE OUT: RACISM, CLASS AND MASCULINITY IN THE 'INNER CITY' AND THE ENGLISH SUBURBS

Les Back

Racism produces a particular kind of urban imagination.[1] In Britain and America the 'inner city' has long been constituted as the key symbolic location for representing racialised criminality, pathologies of black and minority family life and the centre of 'corrosive alien cultures'. Michael Keith has suggested that the relationship between the imaginary/constructed urban environment and the empirical city of racialised subordination 'lies at the heart of some of the most insidious forms of contemporary racism'.[2] The relational symbolism of the interior and external dimensions of the racialised city are mutually dependent on each other. The outer is the locus of white desire, 'the terminus of (upward) mobility,' while the black inner '[is] painted as the bleak, anarchic margin to be avoided, as degenerate space'.[3] At the same time the putative agenda of cultural critics and social researchers has, within their spatial terms of reference at least, shared this geography and anchored the analysis of racism, identity and multiculture within the heart of the city. An unintended consequence of this convergence has been a focus on the presence of the 'racial other' while the preserves of whiteness in suburban hinterlands have been left un-investigated.[4]

The city is not merely an immanent canvas on to which the texts of the racist imagination are imputed. Urban sociality exists as a form of consciousness that is embodied: neighbourhoods that are lived in and produced under particular circumstances (i.e. of state intervention, labour markets, property speculation) but from which emerge 'the social techniques for the inscription of locality on to bodies'.[5] It has almost become a platitude to assert that 'the city' has no essential features. However, I would argue that one can speak of particular patterns of urbanism which provide the arena in which the politics of racism is both expressed and countered. In this paper I want to examine the relationship between class, generation and popular racism and how these articulations are coupled with particular types of urban formation.

It has been established that perpetrators of racist violence are largely young white men between the ages of fifteen and twenty-five.[6] I want to reflect on two periods of fieldwork amongst young white working-class young men conducted in very different urban locations: – one in the 'inner

1. This paper draws from two pieces of fieldwork. The first, in south London, was conducted between 1984-89 and has been fully published elsewhere in Les Back, *New Ethnicities and Urban culture: racism and multiculture in young lives*, University College London Press, London 1996. The second, which focuses on suburban areas in Birmingham, is drawn from a collaborative project with Anoop Nayak and Roger Hewitt entitled *The Social Basis of Racist Action Among Young People in Outer City Areas*. This project was funded by the Economic and Social Research Council (Grant number ROOO234272). I would like to thank the ESCR for their support and also my colleagues, who in different ways have very much informed my thinking in this paper.

2. M. Keith and M. Cross, 'Racism and the postmodern city' in M. Cross and M. Keith (eds), *Racism, the City and the State*, Routledge, London 1993, p11.

3. D. T. Goldberg, 'Polluting the body politic: racist discourse and urban location' in M. Cross and M. Keith, op.cit. p47.

4. Here I am viewing 'race' as an onto-logically spurious concept which is

imputed on social relations and individual identities through processes of racialisation. My concern here is to establish how 'race' is constructed within young people's vernancular cultures.

5. A. Appadurai, 'The production of locality' in R. Fardon, *Counterworks: Managing Diversity in Knowledge*, 1993, p206.

6. Human Rights Watch, *Racist Violence in the United Kingdom*, Human Rights Watch, New York 1997; R. Hewitt, *Routes of Racism: the social basis of racist action*, Trentham Books, London 1996; and L. Back and D. Bains, *Racism Overground: a multi-agency approach to racial attacks monitoring in Birmingham*, BRAMU, Birmingham 1994.

7. Both of these ethnographic projects have also involved discussion of the position of young women, class and gender relations. The focus here is on male youth because of their involvement in overt forms of racist action and violence.

8. In a recent anthology Cohen writes of the strange alliance of social forces which lined up to denounce the new pariah: 'By the end of the 1970s the romantic idealisation of "the lads" (alias

city' and the other in the 'suburbs'.[7] This work was concerned to look at the experience of white working-class young people without portraying them as inherently and uncomplicatedly racist. The essential problem which has guided both of these empirical projects is: how does racism feature within these young lives? What is the relationship between popular racism and the deep-seated transformations which have occurred within the post-war white working class? How can one explore the complexities of young white men's experience without reducing them to caricatures of violent thuggery?[8]

'THE LINE BETWEEN LOVE AND HATE': YOUNG MEN, RACISM AND DIALOGUE IN THE 'INNER-CITY'

In 1984 I started doing field work with young people in two large council estates in south London. The first, which I referred to as Riverview, was initially a prestigious Greater London Council owned estate, which was predominantly white and working-class. The second, called Southgate, was a mixed neighbourhood, owned by the local authority and of a lesser quality in terms of its housing stock.[9] This part of the capital has a long history of migration and had come to represent an archetypal 'inner city' area complete with tower blocks, poverty and urban decline. From the 1920s onwards, outward migration took hold as slum clearance programmes were initiated. Over the twenty years from 1930 to 1950, the local population dropped by 25 per cent. This period was characterised by economic decline within the area's manufacturing industries. However, the decline in population was partially arrested as international migrants from several countries settled in the district.

The largest single group came from Jamaica and other parts of the Caribbean. The settlement of black people in the area did not go unopposed. In 1948 agitation from the National Union of Seamen to stop black people working on British ships provoked a violent confrontation. There was also hostility to black people within the local labour movement. The result was the emergence of a far- right-wing political splinter group which commanded considerable electoral support in the area throughout the 1960s and 1970s.

During this period the number of black people in the area grew steadily. By 1981 black people constituted 25 per cent of the 60,000 people who live in the borough and in some of the districts in the north between 40 and 50 per cent. This population was also youthful. The area divided into a white population that was ageing, as young white people moved out, and a disproportionately youthful black population. In 1971, 45 per cent of people aged fifteen and under were black.[10] In addition, small numbers of people settled from Pakistan, India, Africa, Greek and Turkish Cyprus, and during the eighties, a large number of Vietnamese people arrived.

Young white people in these districts of south London often had an intimate relationship with black-cultural forms of speech and style. In both districts the dialogues occurring within multi-racial peer groups had opened up black-cultural practices to white appropriations. While this process was most profound on the estate I referred to as Southgate, it was also found to a lesser degree of intensity within adolescent communities in Riverview. This identification with black culture incorporated a whole range of social practices from the blazonry of black musical cultures and styles to the adoption of Creole usage and black London argot. Amongst young whites there existed a continuum of identifications with black culture which started with the most rudimentary usage of Creole, to some cases where young whites talked about a stage in mid-adolescence when they expressed a desire to be black. These identifications occurred equally amongst young white men and women. This dialogue constituted in some cases an ethical conversation, often with close black friends and peers, around issues of entitlement, authenticity and belonging. The experience of a young white man called Tony illustrates this point.

When I met Tony he was seventeen years old. He was intimately involved with black cultural practices and in friendships with black peers. He maintained that his use of black talk was legitimate because he shared the same social locations as his black friends:

> I mean people often say I sound like a black man – that is to say I sound black. But you see when I learned to speak English, I suppose it ain't really English, I learned to speak it the way people around me spoke – na mean? I mean when Michael [a black friend] comes up to me and says to me (switches to Creole) 'Whappen Tony cool', I don't answer him with (fakes a public school accent), 'Oh yes Michael I am quite cool thank you'. I say, 'yeah man – safe!' I might not use the talk as hard or exaggerated as him but I'm talking the language I learned to speak, it's – it's my natural language.

Tony is talking here about a social and linguistic space where emergent identities between young people, regardless of background, are formed. However, the boundaries of this process are subject to close scrutiny, as we see in the following extract. It involves Tony and Michael (the boys mentioned above) and Brian. All three boys were seventeen at the time of this incident. Michael and Brian are of Afro-Caribbean origin and Tony is white. The incident took place outside a kebab shop in Southgate. The three boys had just walked out of the shop with some food. There had been some banter between the person serving and Tony.

(All three boys were laughing)
Michael: What did he say to you? Something about . . .
Brian: He said next time he is going to run you out of the shop if you

white male working-class youth) had begun to give way to its opposite – an all too ready denunciation of their inherent and irredeemable racism and sexism. As the 1980s progressed, feminist and anti-racist critiques of "macho street culture" and its "lawless masculinity", focusing on skinheads and football gangs, began to find common ground with New Right diatribes against the "underclass", which singled out unemployed youth as the bearers of a new Yob culture', Phil Cohen, *Rethinking the Youth Question: education, labour and cultural studies* Macmillan, London 1997, p11.

9. The significance of the different status of these estates and the racial discrimination practiced in the allocation of housing is discussed at length in Back, *New Ethnicities*, op.cit., Chs 2 and 5.

10. R. Hewitt, *White Talk, Black Talk: inter-racial friendship and communication amongst adolescents*, Cambridge University Press, Cambridge 1986.

don't give him the money straight away. (laugh)
Tony: You know what I mean, (switches to Creole) **the man chat nuff lyric.**
Michael: (in Creole) **The man was bad rasta.**
Brian: I tell you I think Tony gets blacker everyday! (laugh)
Tony: Yeah sometimes I wish I was black you know. (laugh)
Brian: (Turns and his mood changes) No you don't!

(All three boys stop talking; an air of seriousness descends on the group.)

Tony: Anyway I ain't going back in there again in a hurry.
(All three boys start laughing.)

Tony uses black forms of language in this situation. His use of these symbols is legitimised by his two black peers who allow him access to these cultural forms but also encourage him to be involved in black music and black styles. However, this incident marks the limits of Tony's partic-ipation. Simply, Tony's claim to 'want to be black' is too much for Brian who checks Tony's over-zealous claim. Being close to this interaction, I felt that the boundaries of Tony's relationship to blackness were being defined. In the private context, the presence of racism can be exorcised. But Tony's lack of appreciation of the public prevalence of racism is not reckoned with in his playful desire to be black. This is what offended Brian. When I asked Tony about this incident he said:

> Well, I realised that I had gone too far you – know what I mean. I know I can't ever be black or nothing and I realised that what he was coming off with was right. I mean they go through a harder time and all that – that is to say there are things I don't have to deal with when I am on my own because I am white, but because I am with them, I see what goes on and how people act the same towards me when I'm with them.

Tony's account is interesting because he realises that he over-stretched his relationship with his black peers. Clearly, he understood that there is more to being black than ebullient street styles and prestigious linguistic codes. By adopting and articulating black forms of style and speech Tony was encoding his identification with blackness. However, the contradictory nature of this identification becomes impossible to sustain when it is made explicit. Tony identifies with 'black' symbols but knows he can never feel the consequences of racism and the experiential foundations of blackness.

Accounts of young white people wanting to be black during the period of mid-adolescence are not uncommon. In a sense, these constitute extreme moments of identification but they are continuous with the operation of black cultural forms by young white people. This phenomenon is a curious inversion of academic treatments of 'race mis-identification'.[11] Through these engagements with blackness, young whites are forced to interrogate the meanings of whiteness. They move from the youthful assertion of 'it doesn't matter what colour you are' to a lived knowledge of how racism structures their lives and relationships. What was striking amongst the young white people who had made this transition was the degree to which it had produced an intuitive wisdom on matters of race and racism, and an awareness of the limits of peer identification.

While accepting the idea that non-racist sensibilities are communicated to whites through the process of cultural dialogues, it must also be understood that anxieties and fears about difference are also present, both alongside and sometimes inside these processes. For young white men the imaging of black masculinity in heterosexual codes of 'hardness' and 'hyper-sexuality' are some of the core elements which attract them to their image of black masculine style. This is located around racialised definitions of masculinity. The image of black masculinity as invulnerable, 'hard' and 'bad' is alarmingly similar to racist notions of violent black criminality. At the moment when racist ideas are most vulnerable, in situations where there is intimate friendship between black and white men, stereotypical racial constructs can be coded as positive characteristics to be emulated.[12]

Boy With Football, Woolwich 1989 © Paul Halliday.

11. K.B. Clark and M.K. Clark, 'Racial identification and preference in Negro children' in T. Newcombe and E. Hartley (eds), *Readings in Social Psychology*, Holt, Rinehart and Winston, New York 1947; P. Weinreich, 'Identity diffusion in immigrant and English adolescents' in G.V. Verma and C. Bagley (eds), *Race, Education and Identity*, Macmillan, London 1979; and A.G. Davey and M.V. Norburn, 'Ethnic awareness and ethnic differentiations amongs primary school children', *New Community* 8:1/2, 1980.

12. This point is made starkly by Ned Polsky commenting on Norman Mailer's famous discussion on the 'White Negro': that white hipsters did not want black men to be 'Uncle Tom', but they still wanted them to be 'spooks'. N. Mailer, *Advertisment for Myself*, André Deutsch, London 1961, p313.

13. M. Young and P. Willmott, *Family and Kinship in East London*, Penguin, Harmondsworth 1957; and Phil Cohen, 'Subcultural conflict and working class community', *Working Papers in Cultural Studies 2*, 1972, p3.

14. Tariq Modood has suggested that to stress the newness of this phenomenon is to miss the variegated history of English racism. See T. Modood, 'Difference, cultural racism and anti-racism' in P. Werbner and T. Modood (eds), *Debating Cultural Hybridity: multicultural identities and the politics of anti-racism*, Zed Books, London 1997.

15. This is in contrast to other European cities where ethnic and racial minorities have been located within suburban settings.

16. Anthony King has pointed out for example that the suburban bungalow was 'generated by the interaction of cultures under the conditions of colonialism'. The residential forms comes from India into the West, so in this sense the archetypal suburban house is in itself an expression of organic hybridity. A.D. King, 'Excavating the multicultural suburb: hidden histories of the bungalow' in R. Silverstone (ed),

White identifications with blackness in these inner city settings are ambiguous and complex. Young white men walk a line between an exotic love and desire of otherness which leaves racial stereotypes intact, and a lapse into reactive and venomous hatred of difference. To reduce these relationships to either a parasitic and vicarious desire, or a temporary repression of the 'true' deep-felt racial animus is to miss the point. The ambiguity of what lies in between provides a potential for a reckoning with racism and difference within peer groups that acts as an ethical space in which new forms of socialisation can take place.

This whole process is underscored by the crisis affecting white working-class communities in the post-war era. Slum clearance, breakdown of extended kin networks and physical destruction of the urban ecology of the inter-war working-class communities all contributed to this crisis. Phil Cohen argued that this produced both internal and external pressures on the nature of working-class family life. Isolated nuclear families could no longer call on wider networks of kinship or friends, but had to carry the full burden of socialisation: 'The working-class family was thus not only isolated from the outside but also undermined from within'.[13]

In this context multi-racial groups and youth culture offered an important alternative sphere in which new forms of socialisation emerged. To a greater or lesser extent folk forms of non-racial wisdom or good-sense could thus be generated within peer groups and embraced. It was in this space that whites could claim legitimate ownership of black linguistic and cultural forms. Locally, then, whiteness, racism and national chauvinism were identified as connected in a triangular and mutually reinforcing way. The negotiated access to black practices meant that the former notion of identity could be vacated in favour of a mixed ethnicity which was shared with black peers. This form of identification could not always be sustained, because ultimately young people were brought back and forced to reckon with the meaning of whiteness and the significance of racism in the lives of their black friends. The partial suppression of racism directed against black people existed simultaneously with the application of racist discourses to (for example) Vietnamese young people. The configurations of racism here are complex and unevenly developed.[14]

For all their multi-inflected qualities new and old racisms seemed to have flourished less in the heart of the English city where the 'race problem' had been historically located.[15] What became clear by the early 1990s was that some of the most violent forms of racism were found in the outlying suburban districts. The English suburbs were no less complex in their social composition but what was striking was the degree to which quintessential middle-class images of English gentility and the 'good life' converged with violence, xenophobia and crude racism.[16]

'ROSES AND TERROR': WHITENESS AND RACISM IN THE SUBURBS

Space is all important in the suburbs... There's nothing to do there, nothing to grab hold of except fantasies of self creation.

Jon Savage[17]

The English fight for their territory. If us lot went over there, white people. They wouldn't like it, they threw us out of their country ... Why? Because they're a different colour. That's what it was. That's why we want them out of this country.

Robbie, 15 years old

The suburbs of England's main cities occupy an ambiguous place in the national imagination. Their rose-bushed gardens and domestic splendour serve as an emblem of propriety, respectability and ordinary success; a kind of cultural totem for a nation that seems under threat from the cultural diversity of its metropolitan interiors.[18] However, these areas were also the places where suburban public-housing estates were constructed to receive the white workers who were being offered a privileged residential place outside the inner city. At the same time the white working classes in these suburban contexts were separated from their kin networks and surrounded by sometimes hostile and judgmental neighbours.

The advances in accommodation and newly-found consumer affluence were achieved at the cost to many of their communal institutions. Working-class life in these contexts became increasingly privatised. Vicky Lebeau, in her fascinating discussion of the cultural shape of the suburban council estate, concludes:

What matters is the television as a focal point for a shared looking which somehow binds the mutilated family back together again. Like a prosthesis, the television allows the displaced family to function in the absence of the matrix which had, until recently, governed it, compensating for the loss of family and friends by becoming nothing less than a member of the suburban kinship network.[19]

Loneliness and desolation became the leitmotif of working-class suburban living. Lebeau asks in passing if working-class racism, so often articulated through housing and notions of territory, is linked to the dislocation so vividly described in the post-war literature on working-class family and kinship. This is a point that I want to examine now through a discussion of a second period of fieldwork in suburban Birmingham.

This project started in 1993 with my colleague Anoop Nayak. We began inquiring into the patterns of violent racism in suburban Birmingham.[20] Birmingham is the second largest city in England and has a population of

Visions of Suburbia, Routledge, London 1997, p57; and A.D. King, The Bungalow: the production of a global culture, Routledge and Kegan Paul, London 1984.

17. Jon Savage, sleeve notes to The Sound of the Suburbs (MOODC18), Sony Music (UK) Ltd.

18. It would be wrong to overstate monolithic white-ness of the suburbs. There are several longstanding suburban minority enclaves, the most obvious being south Asian, particularly Pynjabi Sikhs in Southall, West London. Hanif Kureishi has drama-tised the tension between white/suburb and cultural difference in his brilliant novel, The Buddha of Suburbia, 1990.

19. V. Lebeau, 'The Worth of all Possible Worlds' in R. Silverstone (ed) Visions of Suburbia, Routledge, London 1997.

20. This is a compar-ative piece of research which looks at the manifestation of racist action in Birmingham and London. It was jointly directed with Roger Hewitt at the Institute of Education and ESRC funded. Ethnographic work with young people was conducted in two suburban coun-cil estates. The research aimed to

examine the bound-
ary between racism
as a belief and racist
attacks, where possi-
ble and discusses the
transition point at
which racist ideas
become expressed in
actual behaviour.

about one million. Approximately 25 per cent of this population is drawn
from various minority communities, in particular former migrants from
the Asian subcontinent (Pakistan, India and Bangladesh) and from the
Caribbean (Jamaica in particular), with small numbers of Africans,
Cypriots and Chinese. As in other major cities, minority populations are
in large part concentrated in the inner districts.

In order to establish the geography of racial violence in the city we
conducted an analysis of the recorded cases of harassment. Over a three-
year period between 1992 and 1994 the police recorded 403 racial incidents
and the City Council's Housing Department reported 972 cases of racial
harassment. The geographical distribution of these incidents showed some
clear patterns with high numbers of incidents in: a) the inner-city areas
where minorities lived, and b) the suburban wards to the south-west of the
city and to the north-east. However, if one takes as an indicator of risk the
proportion of racial incidents per thousand minority residents a different
picture emerges, with the level of risk of attack increasing for visible
minorities the further away they are from the central wards. For example,
a minority resident of the celebrated inner-city district of Handsworth
stood a one in a thousand chance of being racially harassed during this
three-year period. In contrast a minority resident of the suburban district
of Northfield had a one in a hundred chance of being attacked. This indicator suggested that a minority resident of suburban Northfield was ten
times more at risk of experiencing racial harassment than an equivalent
minority resident in Handsworth. Looking at the city as a whole, the risk
of racial violence took the form of a series of concentric bands which radi-
ated from the central areas where risk of racial violence was relatively low,
to the suburban areas where the danger of violence was very high. From
the police figures it was estimated that over 70 per cent of the perpetrators
in these areas of high risk were young white men between the ages of thir-
teen and twenty-five.

(a) 'The Dean': class community and conflict

The ethnographic research focused on two suburban public-housing
developments; the one I want to discuss here I'll refer to under the
pseudonym of *Kempton Dean*. One of the characteristics of these suburban estates is that they are often given quasi-rural names. Yet to live on a
council estate in England is one of the distinguishing features of being part
of the white working-class. Intense forms of local identity develop around
these housing districts, which constitute the complete social universe for
many of its residents. Abbreviated names are often coined for these
districts which somehow disrupt their pastoral, rural terms of reference
with an injection of intense working-class territoriality.[21] This estate is
bordered on one side by a quintessential English middle-class suburb, and
on the other by open fields and farmland.

21. It is difficult to
illustrate this with-
out betraying the
identity of the area.
New Addington in
south London
provides a good
example of this
syndrome. This
estate is named after
the small Norman
village of Addington
which is located
close to 'New'
Addington, a
sprawling council
estate which houses
30,000 residents.
Young people refer
to the estate as
'Addo', in the same
vein as the vernan-
cular phrase 'Aggro'
meaning 'trouble',
aggravation or
violent confronta-
tion.

The 1991 census recorded that 4182 residents lived on *The Dean* and of this number 98 per cent were white. Opened in the early 1950s *Kempton Dean* was a relatively prestigious place to live compared with the public-housing stock as a whole. Latterly it was a place where a relatively affluent segment of the white-working-class bought in to the political agenda and promise of Thatcherism, where the cut-price sale of council properties took off in the 1980s. A large proportion of the residents were owner-occupiers, numbering close to 50 per cent of the total households. In the 1990s things started to change dramatically. The housing boom collapsed and high levels of mortgage repossession were experienced in this neighbourhood. We might view these areas as a metaphor or indicator for the social transformations that were taking place in the nation as a whole.

The minority presence on the estate, and within the area, is of three kinds. The first is residential. In part due to the lapse of racial discrimination in housing, minorities were gaining access to the previously exclusive estates although the actual numbers were still very small. The 1991 census showed only eighty-six people drawn from minority ethnic groups, and of this small number 42 per cent were African-Caribbean and 43 per cent south Asian. The second type of minority presence is commercial. During the course of the research up to three south Asian shopkeepers have owned premises on the small parade of shops in the centre of the estate. The third type of presence is educational. Due to the greater flexibility on the part of parents to control where their children go to school. One of the consequences of this is that a small proportion of ethnic minority families have opted to send their children to schools in the outer areas because of the perception that they offer a better standard of education.[22]

The patterns of racial harassment on *The Dean* were episodic and took particular forms or styles. Long periods of relative calm were interspersed with intense and focused forms of harassment, damage to property and, on occasion, physical violence.[23] The triggers for racial harassment varied and included disputes between neighbours, the local presence of key violent protagonists and political activity of the far right.[24] The expressions of racism mainly took the form of verbal and physical abuse, but also included orchestrated campaigns of racist graffiti which were targeted at minority homes and the local area more widely.

The south Asian shopkeepers in particular became the focus of this harassment. This is part of the shifting role of the cornershop within the ecology of working-class neighbourhoods. Cohen commented that the disappearance of (white) cornershops in inner-city communities was symbolic of the demise of small-scale economic activity around which much communal activity was organised. This was doubly important since the shop-owners played a vital role in local leadership and in the maintenance of codes of public propriety, particularly amongst the young. In such economic circumstances small retailers can only remain viable

22. This market driven and voluntary form of 'bussing' has been met in suburban schools with unprecedented levels of racism and conflict. During one period of heightened conflict black pupils of a suburban school we worked in were taken home in the school minibus to avoid harassment from a local white gang.

23. These patterns of violence and the forms of local legitimation that accompany them are discussed more fully in L. Back and A. Nayak, *The New Frontiers of Racism: youth, community and conflict in the suburbs*, Ethnic Research Centre for Research in Ethnic Relations, University of Warwick, forthcoming.

24. It is important not to over stress the impact on the local forms of racism of political organisations like the National Front and the British National Party. However, on one occasion the candidacy of a National Front candidate in a local by-election provided the pretext for a extended campaign of racist graffiti directed against a local shopkeeper.

© Paul Halliday.

25. Many white
shop-owners were
not willing to do
this and as a result
sold their business
to hard-working
entreprenuers from
ethnic minority
communities look-
ing to establish a
foothold in the local
economy.

26. This has also
been observed in
Barry Troyna and
Richard Hatcher's
excellent, *Racism in
Children's Lives. a
Study of Mainly-
white Primary
Schools*, Routledge,
London 1992.

through offering convenience shopping, opening long hours and through charging higher prices.[25] In the suburban context, where a small parade of five or six shops service a whole community, the shop itself becomes an intense site of resentment which is often racialised. Asian shopkeepers are viewed as discriminating against whites. As one resident told us 'They even make you pay five pence for a plastic bag'. In comparison with their predecessors Asian retailers are accused of not allowing credit, not waiving small sums, refusing to provide delivery services to the elderly and of over-charging.[26] Particularly in the new contexts of the suburban estates the local shopkeeper went from being a reference point around which communal ties were cemented, to being a symptom of white working-class marginalisation and social dislocation. The complicated economic and political forces which produced this situation could then be reduced to racial scapegoating. The solution, according to this logic, was merely to get rid of the Asian shopkeepers. One piece of graffiti which was plastered over the back entrance to a local Asian-owned supermarket made this plain: 'Pakis Get Off the Dean. It's War'.

Two Asian shopkeepers were in business on *The Dean*. One of the businesses received very little harassment, while the Sikh owner of the main supermarket experienced repeated acts of vandalism, verbal and physical abuse. The proprietor of the supermarket was an extraordinary man. For him the family business was a sideline to his career in civil engineering in which he held a Ph.D. A lecturer at a local university, Dr Sidhou had been the owner of the shop for ten years. Throughout this period he had kept a journal recording every incident of harassment and abuse. In some instances very young boys, around six or seven years of age, were involved but the main perpetrators were between twelve and twenty-five. For the youngsters this involved what Dr Sidhou referred to as 'daily activities of annoyance' including petty stealing, verbal abuse, squirting water-pistols in the shop, or kicking a football against its windows. The older perpetrators were brothers, mothers and fathers who were mobilised to defend the youngsters. He remembers:

> There were numerous times [we were abused], not one. Young kids swearing at my wife in there, spitting at her, spitting at her physically, okay! She tells them off, 'You're not gonna come into the shop anymore'. Then the mother comes up in five minutes, starts an argument with my wife: 'You're not gonna ban my child from your shop. You've got no right!' How would the child react to that? I tried to speak to them ... They don't listen to that. I was attacked twice physically.

Dr Sidhou and his family lived in the local suburb and not above the shop. He also employed some local white residents and young people in an attempt to demonstrate his commitment to the local area. A white woman who worked in the shop told a local newspaper: 'I've been walloped round the head with rolled up newspapers, had footballs kicked at me and my car attacked ... You should hear the abuse we get when we're locking up the shop at night. The language those kids use is unrepeatable and it's all racist'.

From his records Dr Sidhou established that all of the incidents of harassment were confined to three extended families, all living on the estate. Although he reported that some white residents were supportive of his plight, little neighbourhood or communal prohibition was brought to bear on the perpetrators. Like many council estates of this type the overwhelming ethos is to 'keep yourself to yourself – don't poke your nose into other people's business'. This needs to be explained not only in terms of the racial antipathy to the shopkeeper, but also in relation to the deep-seated assault on the working-class public sphere. The intrusion of compensatory and anomic mass culture is part of this process, but it is amplified by the disfiguring human ecology of the suburban estate which reduces social life to the home and nuclear family.[27]

(b) Youth, territory and utopia

The main perpetrators of the daily harassment and racist graffiti were a small group of young men from the estate.[28] This informal peer group comprised of between seven to ten members who were all fifteen years old and 'hung out' around the parade of shops and dominated the local youth

27. One of Young and Willmott's informants, Mr Stirling, captured this sense of limited sociability: 'I don't mind saying hello to any of them, or passing the time of day with them, but if they don't want to have anything to do with me, I don't want to have anything to do with them, I'm not bothered about them. I'm only interested in my own little family. My wife and my two children – they are the people I care about. My life down here is my home', Young And Willmott, op.cit., p149.

28. Anoop Nayak also conducted extensive ethnographic work in the local school where young whites expressed a range of very different positions from the ones discussed in relation to this group.

29. Ironically, the member of the group to be cautioned by the police for writing racist graffiti was one of the young black men.

30. One of the interesting features of the subsequent viewing-was the degree to which the video offered another context to celebrate their extreme racist rhetoric in a playful and narcissistic fashion.

31. The role of play in establishing male working-class autonomy is discussed in L. Back *New Ethnicities and Urban Culture: racism and Multiculture in young lives, op. cit.,* ch. 3.

32. The group really enjoyed the sessions. It gave them the opportunity to speak freely and celebrate their racism to an audience: the video camera operated as a window to a wider world.

33. I was struck in the aftermath of this incident of the folly of trying to bring groups of white and minority youth together for face to face forms of 'cultural exchange'. The danger of such encounters is that they are more like to entrench racial divisions than deconstruct the colour line.

34. The black members of the group participated equally in this

club. To add to the complexity of this situation two members – Calvin and Leonard – were brothers who had one black parent.[29] Through the local youth club we set up group and individual interviews with the core seven members of the group. These sessions were videoed and initially we hoped to play the recordings back to the young people in an attempt to get them to reflect on their accounts.[30] Three out of the seven young people were members of the families identified by Dr Sidhou as the key perpetrators of racial violence. What was immediately clear in the session was their intense commitment to racist views. This was expressed through a fierce localism which constructed *The Dean* as a white area to be defended against the incursion of cultural diversity from outside. The racial zealotry expressed by these young men was impacted and unambiguous.

The performance of racism here was intimately tied up with a sense of masculine bravado, posturing and ultimately enjoyment. To be racist here is both about 'having a laugh' and being deadly serious.[31] For these young men, white supremacy operated as a kind of utopian identity, a means to bring absolute certainty to bear in uncertain times. There was something very telling about the function of racism performed in their transition to manhood. The liminal status of 'youth' was thus managed through an absolute and unflinching rhetoric of white chauvinism, where the mask of the violent racist provide a means to transcend their subordinated status, at least at the level of desire.

One of the things which came out repeatedly in the discussion of the video work was who we were going to show it to. Towards the end of one session Daniel, a skinhead of slight build, asked: 'How come you're filming us?' I replied that we were filming them to record what they had to say. Robbie, Daniel's cousin, immediately responded, 'Show the Pakis what we say'. I told him that we also wanted them to look at the video. A tall white youth called Darren then asked if we could watch the video and I agreed. Daniel turned into the camera and said: 'We hate Pakis, fuck 'em off'. It was clear that the group wanted their video to be shown only to objects of their own fury.

After the video had been shown and I was packing up the equipment, Robbie came back and asked if we could do another session.[32] I said that we could, and then he said: 'Yeah what you should do is bring some Pakis down and we can have a debate. We can listen to what they got to say and we'll tell 'em what we think'. He paused for a moment and then said excitedly; 'Bring some big, dirty smelly Paki down and we can have an argument!' As Robbie walked away I remember feeling as if something important had been revealed in this strange request. For Robbie, this monstrous image of Asian otherness was necessary in order for him to inflate his own 'white selfhood' to the level of an equal opposite.[33]

South Asians were the most vilified group for the young white men.[34] The presence of 'Pakis' in England was used to explain everything from unemployment and lack of housing to general social decline. The young men would engage in a rationalist argument about the truth of these claims, but beyond this the rationale for hating Asians was simply reduced to; 'cause they smell, and they're black, and they shouldn't be in this country!' The groups were also vociferous in their hatred of black people as a group. This included casual and unembarrassed use of racial epithets. This is rendered explicit in the following extract, involving three white youths (Robbie, Mark and Darren), and Leonard who has a black father:

Robbie: Blacks ain't as bad as Pakis
Mark: We smoke their draw.
Robbie: I'd rather hang around with a black than a Paki.
Leonard: Pakis smell.
Robbie: Pakis smell – it's their duty

[...]

Mark: We act like we act and [you] get all the black people, like, walking, swinging their fucking arms like fucking apes.

Darren: We wear jeans, niggers wear cuts in their jeans, pakis wear their pyjamas.

[All laugh]

Here we do not see the ambivalent combination of love and loathing discussed earlier. Rather, the distinction between 'Pakis' and 'niggers' is a matter of the lesser of two evils.

This racial hierarchy was articulated in terms of a belief that people should be 'true to their race'. Mark, Daniel's cousin, summed this up in his contempt for whites who aspire to be black: 'You should act your own colour!' When asked about the two black members of his own group they responded that their black friends were 'all right, because they didn't have attitude problems'. Within the logic of maintaining racial boundaries these friends were ultimately 'half-castes' and in the final analysis, as one member pointed out – 'they're half white anyway, ain't they?' The ambiguous inclusion of Leonard and Calvin was managed by asserting that they were either 'exceptional blacks', or 'really half-white.' The tensions inherent in this proved overwhelming. Soon after we finished conducting the video session, Calvin and Leonard broke away from the group.[35]

The white members all claimed to be supporters of the National Front, although they demonstrated little knowledge of what it stood for. The symbolism of the National Front and more generally of fascism was assimilated into the local grammar of racism. The group had no real ideological or organisational commitment to fascism. Darren claimed to have

rhetoric although this was always in the context of the need to prove themselves in the group. There is no doubt that some of these assertions were deeply felt but in discussion we had with them away from the group these young men said that they were under no illusions that the anti-black racism so widely held could be applied to them.

35. One of the unintended consequences of the ethnography and the 'race talk' it generated was to rendered Calvin's and Leonard's position in the group untenable. A local youth worker told us: 'I think what happened was that you confronted all the contradiction in that group and as a result they couldn't paper over the cracks anymore, or go on like they were just one of the lads'.

36. This is a similar process that Levi Strauss outlined in relation to myth. Here myths are not uniform narratives, but improvised forms which seek to render deep structural contradictions into sets of binary oppsitions. Phil Cohen argued that post-war youth subcultures demonstrate such mythic qualities which express, and magically resolve, the contradictions in the parent culture. C. Levi Strauss, *The Savage*, University of Chicago Press, Chicago 1966; and P. Cohen, 'Subcltural Conflict and working-class community', *op.cit.*.

37. See also Ray Singh's account of similar processes in Keighley, 'Racism and Spacism: racial harassment and localism', *Here and Now*, 141: 46-51, 1993.

38. This would suggest that the culturally inflected 'new racism' outlined by a variety of authors is unevenly developed, and that cruder forms of racism predicated on absolute physical difference have endured alongside new patterns of racialised discourse; see M. Barker, *The New Racism: Conservatives and the Ideology of the Tribe*, Junction Books, London 1981; and P. Gilroy, *There Ain't no Black in the Union Jack*, Hutchinson, London 1987.

the telephone number of a NF activist whom he could call on if there were ever any 'trouble'. For these young men the culture of the far-right served as a symbolic resource which could be invoked to represent 'a racially exclusive localism'. The intense and unmoveable commitment to these positions is hard to over-emphasise. Through their accounts these young people articulated the nature of their plight through a rigid set of oppositions which represented their territory, in contrast to that of the inner city:

Inner city	Suburban
Other	Self
Black	White
Dirty	Clean
Dangerous	Safe

Here they could champion race, and white territory, as a means to find a place for themselves in a situation where white working-class culture and its traditions had all but been erased.[36] As a result these intensely localised racist mentalities offer a sense of heritage and identity.[37] This addressed the immediate uncertainties of lifecycle and the deeper cultural crisis within white working-class life: the magical solution determined to reduce the precariousness of culture to the certainties of race.[38]

In such a situation the rationalist discourses of anti-racism are simply a non-starter: they fail to appreciate the depth of commitment these young people feel to this view of the world. They vigilantly resist any idea of cultural mixture or hybridity, or any idea that their assertions can be punctured by some 'superior logic' or by a multicultural version of history, despite the fact that their language and culture contains these diverse registers. When I asked Daniel, one of the most forthright members of the group, to tell me what he admired about the National Front, he simply replied that it was 'wicked', employing a mode of speech irrevocably branded by its black inheritance.

All the members of the group were fanatical about rave music. We tried to discuss with them the origins of the music in Detroit, where the key exponents had been black and gay. This is an excerpt from a discussion with Kenny:

Les: What kind of music do you like?
Daniel: Rave
Les: Did you see on telly that that was originally black?
Daniel: It weren't.

Les: House music comes from Chicago.

Daniel: Yeah that's house music. It's not hard core.

Les: But you know as well as I do that rave and house are connected, so if you throw black people out you'd have to throw rave out as well.

Daniel: No, because we'll still have all the tapes, won't we!

Rendering these hybrid traces explicit had little effect on this young man's commitment to white supremacy. All urban cultures are highly promiscuous in their endeavours to constantly re-make and invent traditions in the present. However, urban syncretism need not be connected in any direct way to greater tolerance or to a turning away from racism. Daniel's assertion of ownership of 'black culture without black people' suggests that the fact of multiculture need not unsettle racial chauvinism. The assimilation of difference, or new cultural influences, occurs here in unconscious fashion, leaving intact a presumption of exclusive ownership of the culture of the assimilator. The diversity of cultural traces in urban life thus remains latent, mute and opaque.

Locally residents often said that racism was a phase, or something young men 'grew out' of. Cases would be cited of former skinheads who had gone on to lead respectable lives. We recorded incidents of white youth distancing themselves from racism as they moved away from the estate, and into new social domains, many of which were more ethnically mixed. Dr Sidhou was less sanguine about this view:

> Have they grown out of it? No. What they have done, they have changed their actions now. They're not doing the same little petty things that their kids are doing, they've grown up to do bigger things.

The commitment to racism is particularly intense in the period of mid-adolescence. There were some occasions when the peer consensus around racial separatism and conflict loosened, but these were always temporary shifts.[39] They may grow out of these extreme forms of rhetoric, but equally they carry some of the notions of race, territory and entitlement into adult life.

The experience of these young men contrasted the ambiguous dialogues recorded in south London. An overt anti-racist intervention here was likely to generate more racism in response, than to begin a critical dialogue around young men's commitment to racism at this stage in their lives. It has occurred to me recently that it is perhaps better to work on sustaining the non-racialised aspects of their social life than to open up a direct dialogue on racism itself.[40] However, what remains constant in both of the fieldwork settings I've discussed here is that the circumstances I have described are a response to deep structural and cultural shifts within post-war working-class communities. It is to this issue that I want to turn by way of conclusion.

39. During one session we started to talk about mixed relationships. The dominant position was absolute: mixed relationshps were bad. Daniel was sitting in front of the camera in his usual place. Calvin, one of the black young men, pipped up from the back of the group, 'Well what about the time when you told me you fancied Tina Turner?' The consensus in the group shifted. Daniel was ridiculed publically for being 'caught out', and he went from being very vocal in front of the camera to saying nothing, at the very back of the group.

40. I am currently working on an approach to anti-racist work that closely connects the mode of intervention to the social configurations of racism within particular youth groups. In cases like these it might be more appropriate to think through ways of building on the moments when racism is absent, rather than to confront the issue of racism directly.

CONCLUSION

The 'fear of freedom' may have tempted the middle classes towards authoritarianism; it affects the working classes differently. They still feel in their bones that the public and generalised life is wrong. This rudimentary internationalism can co-exist with anti-Semitism ... but such intolerance comes out only occasionally, and the two worlds do not often meet.[41]

41. R. Hoggart, *The Uses of Literacy*, Penguin, Harmondsworth, 1957, p94.

[The white working-classes'] economic position excluded its members from entering the artificial paradises of the new consumer society; at the same time changes in the production process itself have made the traditional work ethic, pride in the job, impossible to uphold. They had the worst of all possible worlds.[42]

42. P. Cohen, 'Subcultural conflict and working-class community', *op.cit.*, p10.

The intense way in which the young men from *The Farm* embrace racism cannot be adequately understood as some 'new' form of yobbery, or evidence of the emergence of a new suburban underclass. Rather, I would argue, it is the ritual expression and resolution of a deep sense of crisis within a working-class culture that has been unhinged by the process of individualisation, anomic consumerism and geographical dislocation. As the skin of the old, suspicious and at times internationalist working-class ethos was removed what emerged was a nascent commitment to the certainties of race. The damage done to working-class communities in the post-war era is not merely about the destruction of neighbourhoods and the undermining of patterns of family life: it is also a matter of the dissipation of their history. Here in the suburban contexts of Birmingham, London and elsewhere the consumerist present won out over the memories of the past. As Roger Hewitt has pointed out, the generations that followed were born into a group with no history and few cultural resources comparable to their black and Asian peers being valued and celebrated by in multicultural education initiatives.[43]

43. R. Hewitt, *Routes of Racism*, *op.cit.*, pp37-43.

Growing up on a council estate in the post-war years provided the key index of white working-classness. Even as the public-housing stock was privatised in the 1980s, 'the estates' remained as a locus of identity formation. Class relations here took on a particular urban form and provided the arena for racialised community politics and the resulting struggles over minority entitlement and legitimate belonging. These strange combinations of suburban gentility, poverty and violent racism have become the enduring legacy of both post-war labourism and the Thatcherite vision of a property-owning democracy. Both of these otherwise contrasting political movements have contributed to the privatisation of working-class culture. In many respects the fortunes of these suburban housing estates provide an apt metaphor for the legacy of Thatcherism.

As working-class residents had their mortgages foreclosed, they cast around for people to blame. The echo of authoritarian Englishness, so powerfully articulated in Thatcherite rhetoric, offered one way of making sense of the situation. For young men in particular the presence of the Asian shopkeeper and newly-housed black residents provided an all too easy means to interpret the cause of the decline in the local economy and housing market. Economic re-structuring meant that Fordist modes of production were replaced by a service economy, which had little need for the older connections between labour, pride and manliness. Young men are faced with a dilemma: Who are they in a situation where their identity is not defined by their relationship to work? Race provides a means to resolve these contradictions and to express belonging, entitlements and identity: 'It's the Pakis, the Niggers that have taken our jobs – This is our country!'

It is a cruel irony that this crisis is most intensely felt in the very places which were intended to offer material advancement and progress, the suburbs. Equally, it is telling that extreme forms of racial attack are increasingly suburban.[42] Racial violence has been effectively suburbanised along with the hollow promises of embourgeoisment, home ownership and consumer pleasure. Perhaps we are only just now seeing the full consequences of the shifts in white working-class culture which commentators like Richard Hoggart, Michael Young and Peter Willmott signalled forty years ago.

It is the inner city, for long the focus of concern about the 'race problem' in England, which has provided a context where these changes have been resolved in less violent and xenophobic ways. Fragile re-negotiations took place in the inner London neighbourhoods which muted the public expression of racism. The urban ecology and community history of these districts produced contingent forms of inclusion which blurred the colour-line. Viewed from outside as 'alien' and 'lawless' enclaves these neighbourhoods are positioned in a very different way within the national body politic when compared to their suburban counterparts. Yet even here, emergent forms of local inclusiveness could co-exist with the exclusion and harassment of newcomers. In south-east London Somali and Vietnamese refugees have been targeted for abuse by groups of perpetrators that are strangely multicultural in composition. While enduring shifts in the cultural landscape have in large part inhibited the open expression of violent racism, new patterns of conflict emerge as old ones are muted.

The spectacle of violence and racial conflict in the English suburbs challenges many of the assumptions that have been made about the nature of the relationship between racism and urban life. In England, and perhaps elsewhere, it is no longer enough to focus our attention on the areas where minorities live as the arena in which issues relating to the plural city are played out. In short our understanding of the geography of popular racism needs to be turned 'inside out'. This involves returning to some of the fundamental changes that have occurred within white working-class life and English urbanism as a whole.

RHAPSODIZING BLACK: HARLEM IN LONDON, 1997

David A Bailey

From 19 June to 17 August 1997 the Hayward Gallery in London hosted a major retrospective exhibition on the Harlem Renaissance of the 1920s, which took for its title Rhapsodies in Black: Art of the Harlem Renaissance. *The exhibition was jointly curated by David A. Bailey and Richard Powell. A catalogue of the exhibition was published by the Hayword in conjunction with the Institute of International Visual Arts and with the University of California Press. The following interview with David Bailey was conducted at the Hayward Gallery by Bill Schwarz on 26 June 1997.*

Bill (BS): Could you say something about the organising ideas behind the exhibition?

David (DB): In 1992 I was working in Birmingham with the photographic magazine *Ten.8* and I produced a publication with Stuart Hall called *The Critical Decade*, which was a reflection on the 1980s as a significant moment of black artistic productivity. When I left college in 1984 I met up with Sonia Boyce, who was a painter, Derek Blackwood, who was working in theatre, Stuart Hall, Karen Alexander, a film maker, Isaac Julien, also a film maker, and Kobena Mercer. There was a time during the mid-1980s, when there were a number of people who were coming out of the colleges, community groups, all areas of cultural activity, who were thinking about the idea about being black, about being British, and who were also beginning to produce works which were of an autobiographical nature, about art history, and who we are in this country. So I was already concerned about the notion of the formation of a black British renaissance.

Shortly after, in 1993, I saw a television programme on Jacob Lawrence. He is one of the foremost American painters, and is also the last remaining survivor of the Harlem Renaissance. The programme showed that for the first time his *Migration* series was being put together, and I was interested in this for two reasons. The first is that the notion of migration is something universal, and is something I saw as a metaphor which enabled me to talk about my parents in Barbados coming to England, and about the whole notion of Caribbean as a diasporic culture – even though Lawrence himself was principally concerned about journeys from the South to Chicago or New York. Also, I thought here was somebody who was working in the format of painting, yet his painting carried textual, even filmic narratives. Here was someone who was crossing areas of cultural identity but also areas of artistic practice. This led to the idea of doing an exibition on the Harlem Renaissance. We brought in, as the key person who intellectually framed the show, Richard Powell.

BS: An exhibition on the Harlem Renaissance had never been curated in the U.S.?

DB: No. And I asked what that would involve, and he said: 'Breaking up the stereotype idea of Harlem being at the centre of this artistic productivity, we have to include people who worked outside Harlem and came in after the key renaissance period'. We also neeeded to include different media: book covers, film, theatre, not strictly related to the visual arts. And we decided to include white artists. There was a moment which was not so much galvanised by a black artistic group but was an actually shared – black and white – collaborative moment as well.

This was in 1995. I was into the idea of doing something that was crossmedia. At the same time I was into the idea of putting together black and white to talk about a notion of international identity.

What's important is that the show has been originated from a British conceptual framework, not an American one: it has been framed in this country from ideas from people in this country, but also it is now going to go to America; we framed that particular history within our own experiences.

BS: You've made the connection between the renaissance in Harlem in the 1920s and the black cultural renaissance in Britain in the 1980s – can you say more about how you see those connections working themselves out? How did Harlem exist in a black imaginary in Britain in the 1980s?

DB: There are two things. When you talk to Stuart Hall, Isaac Julien, Karen Alexander, Sonia Boyce, it's clear that they have been influenced by Afro-American aestethic and cultural practices, specifically by Harlem.

Secondly, one has to talk about the spirit of collaboration, and the spirit of how one finds a particular cultural identity in a sea of whiteness. All these people were trained and taught in white institutions by white people. That begs the question: why, then, do these people come out of these institutions with work which isn't in any simple sense about resistance. It is autobiographical. Yet we've been able to use white institutions and collaborate with a range of white people to produce a new level of thinking about cultural identity, and in turn use this as a resource for creating a black cultural agenda.

When you think about Langston Hughes who tried to produce a magazine called *Fire!!* which failed, he only came to survive under the patronage of white institutions, such as the Harlem Foundation. There is a parallel here to London in 1980s. The Greater London Council was a patronage institution for a lot of young artists, and I think one has to go back to looking at the earlier intellectual work of people such as Robin Murray – and talk about enterprise culture in a way to include these people. This framework allowed a lot of us to come through, and I felt that it was very similar to the economic and entrepreneurial framework of the Harlem Renaissance in the 1920s and the 1930s.

BS: That would suggest more of a shared sociological history than a particular commitment to a specific aesthetics or politics?

DB: It's both. Certainly a shared sociological history, but also a commitment to a political idea in terms of a way of seeing how black and white can contribute to a renovation of culture in England.

BS: To bring it back to specifics in terms of the exhibition, when you were selecting the work in collaboration with Richard Powell, was there any question of how you balanced the sociological factors with the aesthetic ones? Who was included and who was excluded? Did you have a particular thesis you wanted to pursue? Maybe some works were chosen because they were representative of an argument, and maybe there were other works, even by the same person, that were more idiosyncratic and didn't necessarily fit.

DB: The project was conceived as a thesis. When we first came together, we never said we needed to put together an exhibition for the Hayward Gallery; we came together to think more freely how we could do this project. Within that we came out with a whole range of ideas and issues and a whole range of artists. I was keen to show Jacob Lawrence, who had never been seen as part of the Harlem Renaissance because people said he arrived too late, as it were, in the 1930s.

BS: Has his work ever been shown in this country?

DB: No. It was clear that we had to think of a way in which that could be included in the thesis. In one way Lawrence himself highlighted the international dimensions of Harlem. For example many people were interested in Haiti. Josephine Baker was interested in Haiti when she made the film *Zou Zou* and talked about her 'beloved' Haiti. We also thought about Robeson's interest in Haiti, and how he drew on these ideas for his performance in *The Emperor Jones*. Orson Welles based his *Voodoo Macbeth* production on culture in Haiti. When we met Jacob Lawrence he confirmed this centrality of Haiti to us. He had never been to Haiti: yet his first major series, at the age of twenty-one is not about Harlem, coming from the South, it's about something outside Harlem, the Haitian revolution.

Then we had to think about who we could then sell this project to. Originally we thought it would have to be the Hayward. It could have been the ICA or the Serpentine or the Whitechapel. In the end we decided it had to be the Hayward, because we were making an argument that went against the political discourse and art historical knowledge about the Harlem Renaissance, and we felt it had to be contextualised in a space that was seen as the vanguard within the visual-art arena.

But to go for the bastions of the art-historical world produced some unexpected dilemmas. We were keen, as I've said, to include both black and white artists, but we got a sense that custodians of British cultural traditions were wary about big-names British artists being positioned too closely to the influences of Harlem. A lot of people, for example, were suspicious about our decision to include the work of Jacob Epstein. Yet he was, in his own way, not only present in Harlem, but for a time powerfully influenced by the commanding aesthetics of the Harlem Renaissance: in fact he is an interesting exemplification of the cosmopolitan cross-currents of Harlem, which is precisely what we wished to demonstrate.

BS: But his position on Harlem was very ambivalent.

DB: Yes, yes. But because he's white, people think: why include him in the show?

The same reason for Jean Renoir, why have him in the show? Renoir was in Paris, and many black artists went to Paris from Harlem. Renoir met Josephine Baker and other black dancers. He was very much influenced by their work, and he decided to make a film based on his meeting with them, a short science fiction film called *Charleston*, which we're showing in the exhibition.

The same with Orson Welles. *The Voodoo Macbeth* was his last big theatre production, a production that led him to set up Mercury Productions, which then led to him going into radio, film, and *Citizen Kane*. What we're saying is that there was a moment in the 1920s and the 1930s when white artists were beginning to position themselves in relation to black artists such as Aaron Douglas, Jacob Lawrence, and Lois Mailou Jones.

BS: How do you hope this exhibition might be received and read by the people that come to it?

DB: We're talking about visibility, we're talking about decades, even more, when black art has been excluded from the modernist movement. This exhibition shows for the first time that there were artists who were working at the height of their creative powers in the 1920s and the 1930s. But this was the moment when people were beginning to define a particular type of modernism within which black people had been excluded. For the first time in this country, we try to show the centrality of black aesthetics to the history of modernism.

BS: The exhibition shows that it's not just creating a new black modernism; by including works by white artists, including Epstein, it offers a kind of case-study of the white ambivalence towards black culture. It shows that mainstream European modernity itself was predicated on a knowledge and subdued sense of blackness, that it was actually there even when it wasn't spoken. However displaced and subdued in the histories it is, it is a presence. It's like Toni Morrison's demonstration of the mechanisms by which white American literature is in an unspoken dialogue with the black presence. I thought that when you were talking about the 1980s and the black British cultural renaissance, you were going to talk about the way in which black culture actually exploded into the light of day, how it became centred in the public culture of the nation.

DB: Yes. I can talk about this again in terms of black and white. Let me ground it in terms of my own academic formation. I studied sociology, from Sir William Collins in Somerstown to Sussex University, and it was only in my last year that I came across two people. David Mellor, in English and American Studies said to me: 'Why don't you think about ways you can use sociological writing to talk about particular representations of race?' At the same time Homi Bhaba had just written 'The Other Question', which introduced psychoanalysis and Fanon. Even in what was by then a fairly traditional academic discipline, there was an enormous creativity when it came to matters of race and ethnicity.

There were a number of people who came together – black *and* white – who overturned the whole situation around sociology in relation to race, deviancy, urban development. That to me is another indication of the scope of the black renaissance in Britain in the 1980s.

BS: One reflection that relates more to history than to sociology, and to what you were saying about Haiti: given that what you are trying to do is open up and internationalise the sense of what Harlem represented – that it wasn't just a few square miles of Manhattan, but a core of a much more expansive, creative complex across the Atlantic; and given that you're interested in the London/Harlem axis rather than the more conventional Paris/Harlem one, I found it extraordinary that there was no CLR James. The way in which he imagined Haiti, first of all in his play of 1936, with Robeson in it; and then two years later in *The Black Jacobins* – it conforms precisely to the larger culture which the exhibition reveals. After all, Robeson met Eisenstein in a bar in Harlem, where the deal was struck to make the movie. But on the one hand James himself had been formed in a Trinidadian literary renaissance, while on the other, in the British context, he was the figure who connected the black politics of the 1930s to the later generations in the 1980s who determined to cast themseves as black British.

DB: You're right. Time and financial constraints have not allowed him to be more present. But the exhibition travels to the States, and I am now looking for, and I think I've found, the test screening that Robeson did for Eisenstein.

I spent some time with James during his last years, and he informed me a lot about my Barbadian heritage, and my Caribbean roots. The exhibition is still Afro-American focussed. When you look at the Caribbean connection, with Edna Manley and Ronald Moody from Jamaica, it's only a small representation. That's something I personally feel that we need to expand.

BS: I think there's a political issue as well, because what James did, which Robeson couldn't do, was to cut through the whole issue of primitivism, and he was able to do that *because* of his Caribbean background. His famous formulation of the 1930s was that the people of the West Indies are a modern people in an underdeveloped society. He rejected all those discourses of primitivism: he just seems to leap over it in a way in which Harlem and Robeson weren't able to do. It makes James a much more contemporary figure than some of the others.

DB: People have asked about CLR James, and why there wasn't more about Garvey. But people have been embracing the work; for the first time work that was seen on paper has now been seen in real life. We are getting phone calls from American airlines who are wondering about the exhibition, because so many Americans are coming over just to see the Aaron Douglases, which have not been exhibited for fifty years.

This is the first time I've worked on an exhibition where a majority of people who have come to see it have been art historians. At the opening we had 4000 people, the majority of whom were art historians. Also this is the first time I've worked on a major exhibition where most of the major collectors, private collectors, are black. We had a dinner for all the lenders, and I was shocked that here were black lenders who have an interest in that heritage – these are people who collect on a big, big scale. American collectors. I was astounded at the discussions they were having, because they were more concerned about who owned what, so that they could purchase the works. This is something we don't have, except for the Saatchis who now collect a lot of black art from this country. But we don't have a serious body of black collectors. That's really introduced a new debate in this country.

There have been bus-loads of students from art colleges and art education institutes, and plenty of children. It's been a revelation.

BS: I'd never seen Jacob Lawrence, it was just fantastic.

DB: And he came: to see him in the flesh was incredible.

TRESPASS 3: AN ART PROJECT

Sunil Gupta

This project was the third in what I am planning as a series of works exploring and challenging notions of alien presences in Europe. There is a common misconception that art history, as we learn it in schools and colleges and as we perceive it in the culture that surrounds us, is exclusively shaped by a dominant European discourse. My concerns lie around the notion of the New Europe, given the concrete realities of migrant cultures and the hegemony of Eurocentric cultural traditions. Are we as aliens going to be allowed to *trespass* on the cultural terrain of the new Europeans? These days, when 'ethnic cleansing' and other such terminology has become commonplace in our 'objective' media, how do we make interventions and avoid becoming onlookers in the shaping of our own destinies? The work is trying to break down assumptions of the purity of cultural history.

'Trespass 3' originated in images made/found within the county of Essex.[1] The process of the work and the materials used reflect contemporary society in so far as the dyes and paper used in this project have come from commercial printing processes and the images only exist as electronic information in digital code, with the potential for endless manipulation, multiple copying and the lack of an original. The final works could be on paper, could be projected as either slides or computer video projections. The images could be stored on CD or on a variety of electronic storage media. My preference is to present them as ink-jet prints.

In 'Trespass 1' I presented eight mural-size images based on material photographed and researched in Berlin and Frankfurt. The presentation was funded by the project 'Trophies of Empire' and by the Yorkshire and Humberside Arts Board.[2] It was the basis for a solo show at the Contemporary Art Gallery, Vancouver.[3] The images made reference to the problematic presences of Africans and Asians in Germany and in German history. I chose Berlin as a good starting point for my project as it is the capital of the new Germany, the New Europe. 'Trespass 1' was also selected for the 5th Havana Biennial, Cuba 1994, and Ludwig Forum, Aachen, Germany. 'Trespass 2' was commissioned by Frank Wagner of NGBK, Berlin, as part of 'They Call it Love' (1993), a group exhibition. The works for this series were based in my kitchen in London and made extensive references to domestic life and ways in which diverse ethnicities manifest themselves in terms of food and drink.

The original ideas for this project were married to a sense of place and its history. I was interested in tracing the ownership of shares in the East

1. The work was made as part of the 'Essex Fellowship in Photography', 1995, based at Focal Point Gallery, Southend and funded by Essex County Council.

2. 'Trophies of Empire', 1992, marked the 500th anniversary of the voyage of Christopher Columbus to the New World. It was organised by three venues located in England that were in cities closely associated with slavery: Hull, Bristol and Liverpool. The organisations were Arnolfini, Bluecoat and Ferens Art Gallery.

3. *Catalogue*, edited by Keith Wallace, Director, Contemporary Art Gallery, Vancouver, with essays by David A. Bailey, AAVAA, London, and by Eugenio Figuera Valdez, Curator, Havana Biennial.

India Company, as it was the mechanisms of capital that transformed a favourable trading position into the category of empire. Once public shareholders were involved, the financial success of a private company was transformed into a cultural conquest. Since the research dimensions of the project were lost to the vicissitudes of local funding, the project developed through more sporadic encounters with the county. A period of 'artist-in-residence' at local schools also informed the project and fed it with visual imagery.

The project is not trying to say that colonialism exclusively robbed the colonised of their identities, but rather that the processes of colonisation were based upon a cultural *exchange*, one that has had a profound impact on the lives of the colonisers. While it is obvious that the colonised experienced the change, the changes experienced by the colonisers are more subtle. In the sub-continent, patriots demand the removal of all vestiges of British presence, Hindu fundamentalists are demanding the removal of all signs of previous Islamic rule. It's as if the identities of people today are merely related to this or that specific *sub*-culture – that it's possible to cut out parts and not affect the whole body politic.

Similarly in England there has been a great struggle for the acceptance of ideas that challenge the Englishness of England. The city gent in his suit (of Asiatic origins) as the human face of English capital has sought to retain his place in the world economic order. Overtaken by America in this century the grey suits are trying to maintain their financial control over the rest of the world. Of course it has been much easier to keep the communities who live here quite separate. England is not a country of immigrants; it is more like a country of natives and guest workers. It has often been suggested throughout this century that the removal of alien guest workers from Europe will solve all our problems.

What's overlooked is the way in which African and Asian cultures have informed the formation of Englishness, of European-ness. You can, we know, *deport* people, but not the aspects of your identity that their cultures have informed. The language of trading seeks a universal tongue and the more overt swamping of England and Europe has come not from Asiatic hordes but from America, for the ease of communication has meant that Europe became the first port of call for America's colonising presence. In terms of visual arts and public policies, it is not surprising that, historically, British collecting institutions have only ventured outside European art to America. The NATO-like national identities of modern artists collected by the Tate, for example, seem representative of a hangover from the Cold War.

Having studied in this personal void and monotheistic European art culture in the 1970s and 1980s, and having decided that I and other Black and Asian artists were working in a sort of year zero, some of us turned our backs on the career path of studio art-making and got involved in town hall and local grass roots work. We were involved in making our own cultural history. Some of us met around cultural committees in the Greater London Council and went on to start self-help groups. In my case, the crucial point was the formation of Autograph: The Association of Black Photographers, in 1988.[4] From there it has been a constant struggle between cultural activism and art-making. Having participated in the creation and demise of 'Black Arts' in Britain, it's an ugly moment when we are realising the failure of equal opportunities policies.

With the 'Trespass' project I wanted to address the complex issues involved and my changing relationship to them over a longer period. Fittingly the project had its origins in a larger exercise 'Trophies of Empire', that marked Christopher Columbus' voyage as an immigrant to the New World. I find the European experience culturally familiar, but I also see the determination of European natives not to be penetrated themselves. In Europe, Africans and Asians seem permanently exiled internally as foreigners. I feel we are trespassing in another's domain. What the other does not seem to realise is that it is not in our *bodies* that the alien aspect lies – but rather that the alien cultures have already been absorbed into the host civilisation.

4. Autograph still exists as a client organisation of the Arts Council of England and London Arts Board. It publishes monographs and creates new opportunities for Black and Asian photographers. It is one of the few organisations that works across communities.

The references contained within each work are several. The works are presented as visual statements, and the members of the audience are left to make up their own minds about the narratives hidden within them. Electronic montaging technique is used here to create a third reading from the juxtapositions within the final frame.

The classical Indian dancer with the cannon and power station represents a reverse juxtaposition of power relationships. Where she was once controlled, she is now greatly enlarged. The cannon appears puny and insignificant in front of her. In reality the cannon is guarding the mouth of the Thames, an entry point into the garden of England. An important feature of Essex is that it serves as an entry into England and as such functions as a guardian of the culture.

Various kinds of transportation also play a role in the trade routes between coloniser and colonised, and there are many references in the project to train, road and ship. We see the back of a P&O lorry on the M25, itself a road encircling a cultural centre of the Western world, but we can't be sure of its load. The icon of a classical Indian sculpture suggests that the booty might be colonial cultural baggage. P&O is a name that reverberated throughout the colonies and can still be seen in Cape Town, Vancouver and Sydney. The sculpture is of a dancer. It comes from the temples of Chidambaram in Tamil Nadu, South India, the home of Bharat Natyam or classical Indian dance. It's unresolved whether the dance arose from the sculptured poses or whether the sculptures came from the dance.

'Three Men Murdered', a headline in a local newspaper, refers to a gang-land slaying in the vicinity of Chelmsford. The horrific act is committed in the vicinity of ordinary houses such as the one depicted. Already the murders are fading from our memories just like the atrocities perpetrated in the colonies. The little Indian boy looks back at the viewer, now with some reproach. Can we allow the past to be forgotten so easily? The deaths of two million in the Bengal famine in the early 1940s, or the lack of social development in parts of India, leaving archaic practices in place governed by illiteracy and despair – what memories do we have of them? The Raj wasn't a cosy affair, as TV would have us believe: it was clearly the brutal suppression of a people.

The picture with the word 'Explorer' printed on a bicycle is referring to the way in which the arts and sciences were dragged into colonisation under the guise of 'discovery' and 'exploration'. Children are taught to explore their world in an unproblematic way – in this case with a camera simply recording what they see. The crown features centrally, as this entire enterprise is being carried out in its name. The language of history and geography becomes that of innocent exploration and discovery of 'lands' where the native presence is literally ignored for centuries. Artefacts taken from these places now reside in our museums. Ironically these have some-times, in recent years, been shipped back for visits to their native places, so that the people can enjoy them over there. One such exercise is the British Museum show travelling to India showing Indian artefacts from the Museum's collection to celebrate Indian independence from Britain. Issues of ownership and legitimate cultural custodianship are neatly skirted.

The project has been seen widely and is currently going to be seen in 'Out of India' at the Queens Museum of Art, New York, until March 1998.[5] In a twist of current geopolitics, since India has now been absorbed into the Pacific rim by Australasia, 'Trespass' is discussed in an issue of *Art Asia Pacific*, although the work was made in London and shown in Edinburgh.[6] Everywhere the project is seen opens up new possibilities and contexts for cultural debate. The next series will look at London as a primary site for sourcing visual imagery. I hope to be able to continue carrying out research into the relationship between ownership/trade and empire.

5. YYZ, Toronto; Portfolio Gallery, Edinburgh; Queens Museum of Art, New York; Eicher Gallery, New Delhi; Bedford Hill Gallery, London.

6. Antonia Carver, 'Getting Them Between the Eyes: An Interview with Sunil Gupta', *Art Asia Pacific*, 16, Sydney 1997.

MULTIPLE OCCUPANCIES:
LOCATING HOME BASE

Jayne O. Ifekwunigwe

I. Old story, new testimonies

For My Geordie Grandma and My LeGuan Grandad

They will stay together and play together, now that they both
have legs strong enough to run

Scattered Belongings

I am the descended daughter of both and neither
My forefathers are the so-called intrepid explorers
of the dark continent who stole kisses and cultures
The rusty and the dusty dealers in the Triangular Trade
The hyper-zealots who hopped the fence during the
Missionary Crusades—adding a bit of cream to the coffee
And of course—the chocolate brown Africans who were there

At the same time, the distant drones of my fertile
foremothers in Africa, Europe and the Caribbean lull me
to sleep, but never unconscious

*****

The story is old, our testimonies are new.

In varied cultural and historical contexts, countless terms are employed
to name individuals who descend from lineages which cut across so-called
differently configured and gendered Black/White races, ethnicities,
cultures, and classes: mixed race, mixed heritage, mixed parentage, mestizo,
mestiza, mulatto, mulatta, creole, coloured, mixed racial descent, mixed
origins, dual heritage, dual parentage, multiracial, bi-racial, multi-ethnic to
the more derogatory half-caste, zebra, half-breed, mongrel, oreo, Heinz
Fifty Seven, and most recently Cablinasian.[1] I deploy the terms *métisse*
(feminine), *métis* (masculine), and *métissage* which, I argue, more appropri-
ately describe generations of individuals who by virtue of birth and lineage
do not fit neatly into pre-ordained sociological and anthropological
categories. In England, at the moment, there are a multitude of terms in
circulation which describe individuals who straddle racial borders. More

1. In spring 1997
Tiger Woods, the
youngest winner of
the US (golf) Open,
created a storm in
the United States'
Black communities
when, on 'The
Oprah Winfrey
Show', he denied his
'Blackness', (his
father is African-
American and his
mother is Thai), and
instead claimed
'Cablinasian', which
is his own linguistic
amalgam of his
'Caucasian, Black,
Native American
and Asian' ances-
tries. The fervent
reactions to his lexi-
cal intervention
demonstrate the
fixity of the social
institutions of
compulsory
Blackness and illu-
sory Whiteness and
the ways in which
together they create
problematic and
contradictory public
discourses and
private realities for
métis(se) people.

2. Francoise Lionett,
*Anthropological
Voices: Race, Gender
and Self-Portraiture*,
Cornell University
Press, Ithaca New
York 1989; Marie-

often than not received terminology either privileges presumed racial differences ('mixed race') or obscures the complex ways in which being *métis(se)* involves both the negotiation of constructed Black/White racial categories and the celebration of converging cultures, continuities of generations and overlapping historical traditions. The lack of consensus as to which term to use, the limitations of this discursive privileging of race at the expense of generational, ethnic, and cultural concerns as well as the blatant avoidance of inherent hierarchical power dynamics within and between bi-racialised formations led me to *métis(se)* and *métissage*.

In anthropological and literary terms, *métis(se)* and *métissage* are generally associated with France, French-speaking Canada and certain Francophone countries such as Senegal.[2] In the French African (Senegalese) context, in its conventional masculine (*métis*) and feminine (*métisse*) forms, *métis(se)* refers to someone who by virtue of parentage embodies two or more world views, for example White French mother and Black Senegalese father, or what Senghor would refer to as a 'EuroAfrican'. However *métis(se)* is not exclusively a racial term used to differentiate individuals with one Black parent and one White parent from those with two Black or White parents. *Métis(se)* also pertains to people with parents from different ethnic/cultural groups within a country, e.g. in Nigeria, Ibo and Yoruba, or in Britain, Scottish and English. That is, the term recognises the specificity of ethnicities as they are maintained and redefined within national borders. In a globalising world, one can increasingly claim that there are transnational/multiple migrants who by virtue of their cumulative experiences of travel, education and labour represent cultural *métis(se)*:

> The mixed blood is therefore also of mixed culture – a cultural hybrid as well as a racial hybrid. Persons having a mixed culture may and do emerge aside from the process of race mixture. In other words, an individual may be a cultural hybrid but not a racial hybrid.[3]

Similarly stated: 'The place of my hybridity is also the place of my identity'.[4] *Métissage* is a mindset or a shorthand way to interrogate theorising generally associated with *métis(se)* subjectivities and their relationship to the dynamics of power: ruptures, diaspora(s), globalisation, polyvocalities, heteroglossia, oscillations, contradictions, paradoxes, hybridities, polyethnicities, bi-racialisation, 'belonging nowhere and everywhere', creolisation, mestizaje, 'blending and mixing', polyglot, transnationalities, transgressions, multiculturalism, so-called multiraciality, endogenous and exogenous roots, and multiple reference points.[5]

According to F. James Davis, on a global scale, *métis(se)* individuals occupy one of seven different social positions which are determined by the specific hierarchical meanings attached to race and colour in given local milieux.[6] In the first status position, the *métis(se)* individual occupies a

Madeleine Marquet, *Le Métissage Dans La Poesie de Leopold Sedar Senghor*, Nouvelle Edition Africaines, Dakar 1983; David Burley, et.al., *Structural Considerations of Métis Ethnicity: An Archaeological, Architectural, and Historical Study*, University of Dakota Press, Vermillion, South Dakota 1992.

3. Everett Stonequist, *The Marginal Man*, Russell and Russell, New York 1937, p54; Parminder Bhachu, 'The Multiple landscapes of transnational Asian women in the diaspora', in V. Amit-Talai and C.Knowles (eds), *Re-Situating Identities*, Broadview Press, Peterborough, Ontario 1996 pp283-303; James Clifford, *The Predicament of Culture*, Harvard University Press, Cambridge, Massachusetts 1988.

4. Trinh Minh-Ha, *The Framer Framed*, Routledge, New York 1992, p29.

5. Jayne Ifekwunigwe, *Scattered Belongings:Cultural Paradoxes of Race, Nation and Gender*, Routledge, London 1998 (forthcoming).

6. See James F. Davis, *Who is Black?*, Pennsylvania State University Press, University Park, Pennsylvania 1991, pp81-122.

lower status than either of her or his parents, for example, mulattoes of the Ganda of Uganda, Anglo-Indians in India, and Amerasians in Korean and Vietnam. In the second status position, the *métis(se)* individual achieves a higher status than either parent, for example the mulattoes of Haiti and the mestizos of Mexico. In the third status position, the *métis(se)* individual is a member of an intermediate buffer group with marginalised status, for example the coloureds of South Africa. The fourth status position is negotiated on the basis of social class and colour, for example in the Caribbean, including Puerto Rico and Guyana as well as Brazil and Colombia. The fifth status position is a variable one which is supposedly independent of racial traits, for example in Hawaii. The sixth status position also known as the 'one drop rule' or 'social hypodescent' dictates that the *métis(se)* individual occupies the same position as the lower status parent, as in the United States and, I would argue, in the United Kingdom. The seventh status group entitles the *métis(se)* individual to a position of an assimilated minority, as with individuals in the United States with 'partial' Native American, Filipino, Japanese or other 'racially distinctive minority' ancestry other than Black. The specific requirements for membership in the seventh status group articulate loudly and clearly what is almost always silenced in any discourses on *métissage*. That is, according to social engineers, to be 'tainted' with Black African blood is still the ultimate symbol of biological degeneration.

Many traditional anthropological, sociological and psychological studies have perpetuated the idea that a *métis(se)* subjectivity is a 'condition' which requires psychopathological and victimising theorising.[7] Rarely are viewpoints articulated which normalise and frame *métis(se)* individuals' and their families' lived daily realities from the vantage point of agency and empowerment. In the four part harmony which follows, Shanti-Thomas, Lorraine Ayensu, Folake Shoga and Tunde Jegede provide strategies for transcending enclosures. Their evocative celebrations of multiple and complex subjectivities function as living testimonies which transgress and blur racial, ethnic, national, class, gender and generational boundaries. Their personal, literary, theoretical and poetic discursive interventions point to the many contradictions in state and popular thinking about, race, nation, culture, and most notably – family and home. Each of their contributions transforms conventional British and English notions of place and belonging.

At the centre of this complex concern is the rich marrow of alternative identities created by the recovery and reclamation of interwoven, multi-ethnic and multicultural histories. These re-interpretations and re-presentations run parallel with the master-discourse of biological racism which is predicated on perceived physical (phenotypic) differences rather than genetic (genotypic) inheritances. Moreover, within this master-discourse, there is no scope for differential family forms which emerge from the convergences of different languages, religions, and cultures: –

7. L.R.Gordon, '"Critical Mixed Race?"', *Social Identities*, 1(2), 1995.

that which is frequently subsumed under the heading of different races.[8]

In particular, 'Multiple Occupancies: locating home base', showcases the visual arts and musical practices of four talented individuals, who each occupy multiple indigenous and exogenous spaces. By virtue of lineage, they can situate themselves within at least two specific and yet overlapping historical narratives. However, in Britain and England, rigid and irrational bi-racialisation deems it possible for them to own just Black – not and – White social identities. Nonetheless, their powerful cultural critiques form the foundation for their individual constructions of place and belonging and name each one of them as a dynamic agent actively engaged in the shaping and moulding of their identities. In turn, by writing themselves back into the centres and not the margins of histories, their texts function as heightened representations of the individual and collective angst facing all people living in the (English) African diaspora(s) and beyond.

8. Heidi Mirza (ed), *Black British Feminism*, Routledge, London 1997; Zhana (ed), *Sojourn*, Methuen, London 1988; Carol Camper (ed), *Miscegenation Blues: Voices of Mixed Race Women*, Sister Vision Press, Toronto, Canada 1994; Naomi Zack (ed), *American Mixed Race*, Rowman and Littlefield, London 1995; Maria Root (ed), *The Multiracial Experience*, Sage, Thousand Oaks, California 1996.

Our testimonies are new, the story is old.

*****

Dear Shanti, Lorraine, Folake, and Tunde:
When I see your faces, I cannot help but remember the war.
When we look into each other's eyes, our war-torn souls communicate in their silences.
When we break that silence, we find community, and that is reconciliation.

In Triumph and Struggle,
Jayne

II. Re-naming

1: Portraits of a woman of mixed race
Shanti Thomas

My name is Shanti Thomas.
I am an artist.

THE SEARCH

My paintings document and describe narratives of growth and decay and processes of physical sensations and emotions. That is, my work tells stories, my own as well as others I have encountered. Both my roots and feelings of being rootless appear in the work, especially the early paintings.

Fragmentation of the human spirit is a common twentieth-century phenomenon. Concepts of Diaspora, with vast groups of people leaving homelands, have forced a break with belonging. Identity is then forged by the complexities of acquiring multiple identities and claiming multiple homelands. The question these multiple affiliations raise for others is that they assume our loyalties are in conflict. The questioning of where we belong and to whom has repercussions for migrants and their descendants, because it may appear that in spite of our actions, we will never feel accepted. We are designated 'Others'. For those of us of mixed race, we often receive ambivalent messages from both sides. This dual ambivalence leaves us in a state of total rootless abandonment. I believe the time is ripe to re-address the simplistic grouping of identities based on Black and White sectors. There is now an ever growing-number of mixed-race people forming, who will be a significant voice in Britain and indeed the West.

MY PEDIGREE

> My mother is Italian.
> My father is Indian.
> I was born in London in 1949.
> I am a mixed-race woman.

My parents faced conflict and prejudice from others who did not accept them. When they met in the 1920s, it was shocking to break with White and Black societies' traditions and for them to unite in marriage. Fear of this combination of Black man and White woman marrying and procreating was perhaps in reality fear of the stranger or the other. Boundaries had

The Journey, painting by Shanti Thomas.

been transgressed. Fear of adulteration and weakening of the dominant White group identity and structure followed. That initial suspicion of mixed marriages and of the offspring is disturbing to the masses because we are not necessarily always physically recognisable. For a long period, we have been marginalised in societies. On the whole, we have no unifying group identity, racial characteristics, or cultures that are classifiable. At this point in time, we are at the beginnings of gathering together, exchanging our stories and deciphering criteria for our collective recognition.

My paintings describe my process of self-recognition. This process involved painting pictures that retold my parents' stories after their death in the early 1980s. 'Leaving', a triptych, tells their stories of displacement after being prisoners of war in Italy. This experience left both of my parents ill during my early childhood.

Other work was based in India and depicts the effects of colonialism on Indian Christians such as my father, who was Protestant. My paintings are visual representations of stolen Black identities and severed links with Indian culture. A group of works was based on my journeys to India and Italy. These explorations of cultures and family-ties are what have given flesh to the bones of my identity. Even though my ties are spread out at disparate ends of the globe, I carry these Indian and Italian links with me as sources of internal protection and security.

Leaving, Painting by Shanti Thomas.

To be heard, one has to be an active participant in one's communities. One must not fear presenting one's argument. I have been fortunate in having such rich cultural influences as my wellspring. I would encourage others with multiple identifications to acknowledge rather than to deny these affiliations.

2. I am an Island
Lorraine Ayensu

Island

I am an Island
I have no borders, no check points
I am an Island, surrounded by blue sea

You can swim to my shore
You can rest here awhile
but you won't ever be
This island's refugee

I am an island
I take on waters from all sides
I am an island, surrounded by me

Use me as your dumping ground
leave your toxic waste, don't hang around
and you say you can't stand the tragedy
yet you spoil me emotionally

I am an island, I have no borders, no check points
I am an island, surrounded by blue sea

Drop your anchor, remain off shore
Rush this island and take what you need
When you've had it all, your bare-faced smile is
what I am left

You can't stay
You can't stay

My songs allow me to plot a course and to map out my feelings as time goes by. This is particularly important for me at present because I am spending a lot of time trying to discover the truth about who I am. That is, I am trying to lift the lid on the secret being held by my deceased birth-mother's husband in Manchester. My point of departure is that I live with a contradictory history and identity which do not stem from a conventional sense of family. I was conceived as a result of my White English birth-mother's extramarital relationship with my Black Ghanaian father. She was married to a White English man. When I was 'born Black', my birth became a secret. This secret became a manufactured lie which perpetuated the idea that I had died at birth.

My experiences challenge dominant models of the family. That does not mean that I do not have to break out of boxes. I do have a sense of my history but it is not based on a strong model of family. It is based and rooted in fragmentation. My fragmented experiences give me strength. They no longer scare me. I therefore embrace and continue to work towards further embracing the contradictions of my own identity and history. Whilst I am making efforts to find and connect with members of my natural family, at thirty-five years of age, I do not think I will ever be able to assimilate fully because we do not have a shared history.

It is the difficulty of my personal history that makes me want to discover the truth. My identity assists me in being able or willing to recognise differences. My life has always been about communicating across differences. Fundamental to this crossing of borders is the notion of family. I did not experience traditional family life. I was brought up in White institutions – children's homes and then in a White working-class transracial foster placement. I lived in large groups. I had several carers, many of whom were White.

I have no desire to assume (or subsume myself under) a more easily identifiable, an acceptable Black umbrella. If I try to move away from what is defined as Blackness or being Black and away from assumed, essentialised cultural roots towards my lived multiple realities, then Black people fear that I am denying my Blackness. On the other hand, claiming Whiteness makes White people feel safe around me because they believe I have assimilated. In their eyes, I then become harmless.

My ethnic and cultural identities are strongly rooted in White Geordie (native of Tyneside) culture. Embracing my Geordie experiences involves both a racialised critique of my ironic circumstances and an affirmation of my origins and my complex realities. I am detached from my natural/biological roots and from a straightforward line to follow. I am alone. I am an island. Hence I break away from the notion of a singular or simplified Black/woman/lesbian identity or any other 'dominant category' definition.

I have learned to love my fragmented self because it makes me feel whole. I do not always want to be part of a 'we' group because for me that often means part of me is put aside. Part of me is hidden. For me, actual complex contradictions are safer to live with and to be with than illusions. It is from within this contradictory space that I am able to tell the truth. Contrary to the occasional sentiments of Black people or other Black mixed-heritage/parentage/race people, making space for myself and my 'am-ness' does not mean that I am any less committed to eradicating inequalities on the bases of gender, race, sexuality, class, age or disability. In the company of friends and as a social worker, I demonstrate my social and political convictions quietly.

Claiming space for a fluid sense of myself does not mean that I have abandoned 'the Black cause', nor does this diminish my belief in the importance of education for self-empowerment within 'the Black community'. 'Multiple occupancies: locating home base' has created a primary textual space for those of us of Black mixed parentage to break down established ideas about our existences. Within this constructed domain, in a very personal way, I can describe the ways in which social policies and social attitudes of the day have affected my life's direction. From the moment of my birth, external control by others changed my life's course. Their decisions removed certain choices and created others. However, such born powerlessness has been reborn as resilience. Neither typically 'Black' nor 'White', my music-making is instrumental as an everyday survival strategy.

In closing, I want to say that the less rigid we are about the fluidity of our identities, the more likely it is that we will all survive and thrive. This does not mean abdicating responsibility for history and the experiences of marginalised groups. For myself my 'amness' must be allowed. My sense of myself must be mobile. My identity is forever fluid. I am on a journey where my final destination is unknown.

Eleiyele, by Folake Shoga.

III. Re-claiming

1. The Yam Store
Folake Shoga

When I was researching for my film, *My Father's House*, the late Professor Axworthy's reels of 16mm got me remembering the books. Caroline Axworthy had said, 'Come up, I'll make you some soup, and I'll have a look through Jeffrey's African things'. The soup was pretty good and there in the boxes under the study table were big flat cans with labels: *Shakespeare Festival, Theatre on Wheels 1964, Festival Tour, Port Harcourt, Enugu, Maiduguri, Kano, 1964*. And the images! Of a fresh, precise, fertile and potent Nigeria, rendered in black and white like my family snaps of that time; an innocent giant striding out of the bush, wearing new clothes as yet uncreased by wear. Not like today's Nigeria, a tattered old geezer, ineffectually wandering, pockets leaking oil, minerals, and untold riches. His unruly offspring rip the holes in them wider with their unlicensed grabbing, recklessly spilling abroad much more than they retain.

Seeing the film brought back to mind how, growing up, we expected to be surrounded by contemporary fiction, we would go unembarrassed to poetry readings, see new plays premiered and be aware of the instant political repercussions. The writers we knew of – Achebe, Soyinka, J.P. Clarke, Okigbo – were in fact a very small community, the elite of a super-selective system, who had been to the same schools, read the same books, and whose writings besides were on the same curricula: those we were being taught by. Perhaps it would be possible even now to trace their influence on the nation by a visit to the University of Ibadan bookshop, which still has on display anything not sold out within the past thirty years. Last year I was startled to see a 1966 copy of Soyinka's *Before the Blackout*, no doubt in the same place on the same table it has always been. The bookshop's peculiar accounting system necessitates a whole table top covered in receipt books, one for each publisher stocked. Finding the right receipt book can take minutes. But then, in a country where the only certainty about the electricity supply is that it will be cut off, electronic spreadsheets are not that useful either.

African literature we took seriously, but books for leisure and pleasure were mostly English. Doris Lessing has written of seeing the African reality of her childhood ordered and imposed upon an imaginary English literary landscape, and conversely Chinua Achebe has written of the magical vistas opened up by talismanic words redolent of foreign-ness, a favourite being 'periwinkle'. Certainly in my privileged childhood great swathes of experience were seen through a bookish haze. But the fantasies of Europe communicated to us were imbued with a tint, a taste, by the setting we read them in; given a vividness, a sensory texture, by the tropics, which subsequent experience of the real thing has not been able to live up to. I do remember looks, textures, smells of books: dust, red cloth backboards, squashed silverfish, coarse paper with fibrous lumps in it you could scratch away leaving a little hole, and the imaginary smells, the imaginary tastes, conjured by the story. The smell of the beer, the taste of the grain, the dust of the chaff, in the Grimm's tale of the sparrow and the cellarman; cadences that stayed with you only to be fitted back to their words if you chanced to read the story again – 'not wretch enough yet, quoth the sparrow'; and phrases divorced from the rest of the text, wandering loose in the mind so that you had had such a funny thought – 'she lost an eye in that terrible beating..' (*I, Claudius*).

In our school library were American classics on thin bible paper, smelling of cellulose, that adhered together with such intractable compactness you could only get them to lie open by thoroughly cracking the spine, when all the pages would fall out; banal popular fiction from the twenties, *Beau Geste*, and a host of Ruritanian novels; and a fabulous find which I wish I had nicked, since it has probably been burned by now (that is how old books were culled), a reprint of *The Princess and Curdie* on thick cream paper re-illustrated with 1930s stylishness. One has to wonder who took the decision to pack them up in a box and send them to a mission school in Africa? Some of them one was very glad for, but I still cannot see the logic of it: *The Land of the Lord High Tiger, The Silver Curlew, The Eagle of the Ninth, The River Boy*. At the British Council library, my sister read and re-read the entire works of Richmal Crompton, Jack London and Paul Gallico. Not only Englishness – deliberate word – was absorbed in this packaged, distanced form, but a large part of our own Nigerian culture was acquired second-hand, as an idea, not an experience. An idea which my father and other family members had a more real relation to than we. Also in the school library was a whole pile of copies of *Nigeria Magazine* dating from the 1950s onwards, an archive of custom, dance, politics and costume in plastic-smelling pages and shiny black and white photographs. (I cannot think about the library without seeing again its shiny tiled floor, the labour of polishing it shared out among the boarding pupils, all housework on the campus being part of everyone's daily duty. After washing, sweeping and applying polish, the floor would be buffed with half a coconut husk: a long job for a schoolgirl, but I have seen a young man, all rangy muscles and vigour, finish the job in about two minutes. Men are so suited to housework I wonder why they do not do more of it.)

My trophy books, mostly off my parents' shelves, would pile up under my bed while I scanned for something impressive-looking that would also provide a good read. Many a dull text has a pretty good introduction. I particularly remember Dorothy Sayers' translation of *The Divine Comedy* (correction – the text only became dull when we got out of Hell). The best for my purpose was my mother's economy complete Shakespeare, big as a brick doorstep. With a keen sense of self-publicity, I would carry this up and down the paths of the boarding school, open, reading, on my way to Mass, or to study, or to meals. And I really have not acquired any additional knowledge of English history since all of those Henrys and Richards.

Books I would not have been seen dead with: anything by Barbara Cartland, Denise Robins and Enid-bloody-Blyton. Other books every-body in the boarding house had read: *Punish Lesson*, putting the 'tit' into 'titillate'; *Maria Monk*, anti-Catholic fantasy, featuring nuns, priests, orgies, white-slaving and dead babies and thus of crucial interest to anyone in a convent school; *A Basket of Flowers*, which though it contained flow-ers, saints, mountains, unjust executions and innocent young women, had nothing to do with Faust. Then there were assorted Lives of the Saints, on cheap paper and in obscure language, like poor little Maria Goretti, of whom the local tough demanded that she commit an impure act with him, whatever that might have been. And the real McCoy, missals, which every-body had, redolent of power and mystery. It is a long time since I saw an old-fashioned missal, with its Latin on one page and facing English trans-lation, its red and black print, a call and response starting with the Asperges, its thin, tough, red-edged paper and its mystical illustrations, all robes and sheepish looks and gushing magical blood. The gorgeous language of some of the Marian prayers, novenas and so forth, lost now to my memory except for a few lines: 'Who is she that cometh forth as the Morning rising, fair as the moon, bright as the sun, terrible as an army set in battle array?'

Supposing with all this New Technology they came up with a way of scanning text straight into the brain at ten times the speed of speech – we could call it reading. And a clever piece of hardware with its own power source, so compact you could retrieve the data from it anywhere you cared to go, the toilet for example. We would have to call it a book; not to mention the creation of virtual worlds where you could converse with gods or heroes or completely imaginary people in completely imaginary spaces. Well, I guess we would have to call that one a novel. That quantum leap that we are supposed to be taking into cyberspace, have we not taken it already? Are we not just still stumbling forward from the momentum of the great leap into abstract signification that was writing? By displacing the means of human communication outwards into a detached physical object, writing changed forever the way we speak, think and relate to each other; made illiteracy possible, included economics at a fundamental level into the dynamic between expression, charisma and the artist of words; deval-ued forever not only orality but all the other forms of signification that are not directed towards words. And made it possible for words to travel beyond human presence, over barriers of time, space and language, the written word an instrument of telepathy.

Jeanette Winterson has written recently about *taking* books, a conquer-ing lover. But since such a partner is four-fifths imagination, I would have thought the solitary vice was a more apt metaphor. I am being snide because it is strange to me that she can describe the act of reading as active, virile, the invasion of territory, the conquest of space. To me it has always been more like being taken over, seduced away from work or study or good company, to run with the wraggle-taggle gypsies or with the imperialist wolves, or to consort with the colonial conquerors. For no matter how much fun you are having with Western fiction, sooner or later you will come up against a little piece of grit in the relationship, a little nugget of racism or anti-Semitism, his twin brother, without even beginning to consider overtly racist writers like Maugham or Conrad, as Achebe has done. You could be ambling down eccentric ancestral corridors with Osbert Sitwell, vaulting over the heights of modernism with Gertrude Stein, or romping down the garden with Beatrix Potter: hell, you could be gallivanting with Graham Greene's aunt – and sooner or later, it is that little piece of grit, grown into a great big signpost for the Black or African reader, pointing out our place in the story. And the guilty feeling of collusion, when one has thoroughly enjoyed the narrative, identified with the hero, and admired the action! It has certainly sharpened my antennae for distinguishing what, in the pull of the story, can be most alluring: the dash of sadism, bluster of heroics, the bright lights of racialist superiority and corresponding lure of 'the primitive' that inform that other mainstay of my childhood reading, popular imperialist romances by such writers as Rider Haggard, John Buchan or Edgar Rice Burroughs. Reader as tart, going over to the enemy.

Or reader as addict, restlessly craving the next fix. Or perhaps, reader as bulimic, but without the subsequent evacuation. Once holidaying in England, my sister spent her entire holiday money one mad afternoon in a bookshop, on wares she had almost certainly read most of before. I suppose she wanted to own, touch and smell them, to redraw familiar boundaries round herself in a foreign land, to add a few more bricks to her book tower, another layer to her labyrinth. I saw her library recently, in Nigeria of course, a padlocked shelf-lined room, with her trash books, her comfort-food books, her custard-cream-and jammy-dodgers-type books – science fiction and Georgette Heyer at the bottom; her essential-food books, her pounded-yam-and bitterleaf-soup-with-pomo-and cow-heel books, Mphalele and Ngugi and Achebe and Ekwensi and Laye and Okri and much more besides – in the middle; and right at the top, books and books of criticism. Those would be the caviar. Some of it no doubt written by those gorgeous clever young men I saw once at the Mbari club, who were, as I remember, funny, friendly, witty and kind – I had tagged along with the foursome that day as little sister. Their bodies could have been polished with teak oil, their minds sharpened by a mechanical grinder, products of our elitist aspirational system. And I remember hearing of another boyfriend (not one of the nicer ones: a major characteristic of his published fiction was his total inability to empathise with any female character), so muscle-bound that he would lie in bed cracking the joints in his toes just by wriggling them. England, envy the education system that turns clever people out to be so fit, especially since it devolved from yours in less decadent days!

In my father's house, there are books everywhere. My mother's Reader's Union books, war memoirs, and biographies of people related to Virginia Woolf or Dylan Thomas or Augustus John or Tyrone Guthrie or Laurence Whistler; her home furnishings and do-it-yourself and old-time tropical survivalist books: how to cover a sofa and make a stout pair of mosquito boots from the left-over fabric; how to make mock peach jam from green paw-paw and mock cream from tinned butter and powdered milk; how to make fitted cupboards for a whole kitchen and a child's desk from the scraps (and she did); how to teach yourself to play the violin; how to educate your child at home (which she also did); a dream of Festival of Britain meets the Pioneers. My father's books, of which his favourites are in a cupboard in his bedroom: biographies of African or Third World statesmen, or prominent socialists; histories of the Sudan; sympathetic missionary accounts of West African peoples from a hundred, two hundred years ago; anthologies of West African voices through the centuries on various topics, say trade; analyses of current affairs; anything to do with Nigerian culture and history; and a lot of Primo Levi. All through my childhood, an acceptable birthday or Christmas gift for him was one of Simenon's innumerable mysteries, but none has made it to the bedroom cupboard – which contains a dream of a new socialist West Africa, rooted in a knowledge of our rich complex past, of the pattern of ripples that crossed the Sahara, the Atlantic. Downstairs, in his study next to the kitchen, his cases of old physics and chemistry textbooks, and scientific journals from the 1940s and 1950s, and government reports, and old copies of *Time* magazine and *The Economist*, and forty years worth of official letters and our old school reports, are overlaid now by stores of a more essential nature. For in these poststructural adjustment days, everything that is liable to walk out of the kitchen too quickly is locked away and doled out. Soap, toilet paper, grey detergent that does not work, gari, sugar, palm oil, ground nut oil, powdered milk, onions and great crusty yams show the encroachment of an earthy necessity into our dreams of detached intellectualism.

And as a last word, yams also featured in one of Axworthy's films. During one of their tours, he must have taken a walk through an Igbo village. There was an old decaying Mbari house, ghostly and immanent on the silent film, and there was a yam store, row upon stacked row of knobbly tubers, pushing through the palm fronds that shaded them. Large, long, round-ended, rough, full of essential carbohydrate, stacked on the ground in that thirty-year-old sunlight, imposing their organic irregularity onto the system of lashed-together poles that structured and quantified them. They made me think of a store of breasts. It is an awkward metaphor: their roughness, their physicality, the multiples of rounded forms. To make such a comparison, you need a very different image of the body from the one forcing young girls into anorexia. (I might look down and fancy that heaviness, not to say lumpiness, with which age and gravity endow the body, similarly signify a substantial nourishment – a token of physical and mental fulfillment – but even as an example of wishful thinking I would not expect clever young women from academies to have the least bit of sympathy for that idea.) As to the yams, one could trace, in the crumbling earth adhering to bark-like skin and in the cobwebbed remnants of root tendrils on fat dark bodies, forensic evidence that alchemical transmutation – energy to matter and back again – is an earthy, basic business; a business that will get feet dusty, fingernails black, an aching back and itchy legs. And one can imagine writing as an act of farming the mind, and reading as the laying-up of fertile tubers within the imagination, tubers whose intractable substance keeps spilling over whatever tidy compartments one chooses to array them in.

2. Cultural genealogy within the African Diaspora and how this is reconciled with a bi-racial identity

Tunde Jegede

I have always considered the contextualisation of one's own work as crucially important both in terms of culture and race. The effectiveness

of art is not only its delivery, but also its reception. The receptive mind of an audience is inevitably coloured by its cultural indoctrination and social conditioning. In Britain, more often than not, people's questions in relation to my music and instruments have far more to do with race and geographical location than with the actual art of music. For me, this is most evident in my interaction with people in the circumstances of having studied and performed on instruments from two very different legacies and systems of learning. These exchanges leave me in a position of continually having to witness and observe people's engagement and treatment of these instruments according to their creator's racial origins.

It was as a result of an awareness that most visual representations of me with these instruments have political significance that I deliberately create images which counteract established preconceptions. Because of this trait many people, particularly in the media, find my images disorienting and sometimes disturbing.

The photograph of myself with the Harp-Lute (Kora) was intended to embody an African Formalism which I am familiar with but which is rarely accentuated or presented in the West. This is reinforced by the sculpture representing the Old, while the clothes were chosen to portray a Contemporary Urban African Diasporic Aesthetic. The image with the Cello was to present the refinement of an artist who is of African descent. It continues with the idea of juxtaposing the symbolism of Old and Modern, for the jacket echoes Elizabethan and Renaissance costume, but it is placed within a Contemporary context.

What these photographs illustrate is the importance of identity and the ways in which this dynamic can be expressed and portrayed by artists in all its dimensions in any sphere of their work.

My identity

My identity is defined by obtainable facts. I was born in Britain and I am therefore a British citizen by birthright. My father is a Yoruba from

Nigeria and my mother was born in Britain of English and Irish ancestry. The diversity of my parentage is highly common to most human beings on the globe at the moment. Therefore, I would not consider any label signifiying 'mixed' parentage to be a relevant classification for me. The crossing of peoples and racial groups has been going on for thousands of years, since pre-Biblical times, making any claims of so-called 'purity' ludicrous in our era. The only genealogical area of scientific factual weight is the recurring genetic traits of particular bloodlines.

These descriptive categories which attempt to define my genetic make-up and identity do not correlate in any significant ways to the genesis of my musical or artistic compositions. However the cultures which I am versed in do influence heavily my creative language and processes. I studied the West African Manding tradition of the Harp-Lute and the Cello within the European Art music tradition, which makes me versed in these two cultures.

The presence of an African Diaspora in the West has not just shaped culture for people of African descent, but inadvertently the African Diaspora has actually been the stimulus for twentieth-century Western culture. When we recognise the profound influence of the century, of African art on Picasso or of African-American culture on composers from Dvorak, Delius, Ravel, and Stravinsky to Stockhausen it becomes clear that this has been a century of the African Diaspora, albeit unacknowledged. This disavowal occurs even before we begin to address the arena of popular forms of music. I am confident that the African Diaspora will continue to be at the forefront of culture in the twenty first century, but this will depend solely on the continued renewal, rejuvenation and regeneration of forces within this cultural canon.

Songs of the eternal – solo cello

In many civilizations in the East, music has always been understood to be an art of invocation and spiritual worship of the divine as well as being part of the expression of human existence. The idea of our gradual evolution is a result of the linear and progressive perception of time currently held by Western civilizations. The concept of an 'Eternal Now', an impulse ever-present and simply retouched and restated, is one which originated in the East and was a perspective held by many civilizations of Antiquity. It was only with the introduction of measurements and rational reductionism that fixed concepts of time emerged and the present became a mark of the moment and a dividing line between past and future.

It seems Western civilization has been drawn to the worship of reason and intellect of the conscious mind as the divine, inherent in the developed man and woman. Thereby, understanding of the progressive evolution of humankind is from the so-called 'Primitive' to the sophistication of the 'Modern'. I do not adhere to this understanding of the 'Ancient' and I believe that humankind was originally created perfect, fell from grace, and through the stages has been trying ever since to regain position. It is for this reason that this piece opens using harmonics from the 'Natural Harmonic Series', which is the scale in harmony with the principles of the Natural Archetype, before the evolution of Bach's well-tempered solution which enabled keyboard instruments to play twelve keys concurrently. As a composer and a creative musician, my impetus is to honour the Prime-Archetype as the divine and eternal wisdom and light of the ages – hence, 'Songs of the Eternal'.

Cycle of reckoning – Harp – Lute (Kora)

'Cycle of Reckoning' is the expression through music of the metaphysical journey made by millions of Africans across an unknown sea to an unknown destination, and their experiences on arrival. It is a history which has been both neglected and ignored, but it is a past which cannot be resolved until it is faced and understood. In light of the conflicts and tensions which still arise in many inner cities of the Western world today, this history is still relevant to Africans across the Diaspora.

'Cycle of Reckoning' is a reflective piece with an imaginary, elusive figure looking back over his life's experiences, which are symbolic of a betrayed Nation. There are seven distinct sections, but the work is not divided into movements and the music runs in continuum from start to finish:

1) 'Introduction'
   This section opens the musical world of this piece and sets the scene for the epic journey upon which we are about to embark. It establishes a surreal calm before the first thought and impulse of human expression from within.
2) 'Africa I Remember'
   Here we are introduced to the relentless spiritual heartbeat of a people who will have to endure insurmountable odds. It is the strength of this integral spirit which carries them through. We see this resolve in many guises, sometimes in the form of bitterness and sorrow and at other times as resistance.
3) 'Capture and Realization'
   These passages look at the conflict and tension between resistance and resignation and the realization that both are necessary and needed, but at the right time. It portrays the undercurrent of those dark forces which underlay and perpetuated this episode in history.
4) 'The Middle Passage – The Crossing'
   This section illuminates the tragedy and dissonance of the journey. In order to draw out an empathy and humanity towards a particular people's plight and replace the present state of indifference, it acknowledges a horror which is difficult to conceive.

5) 'Arrival'

This is a celebration of the indomitable spirit which will overcome the insurmountable odds of the New World and adapt to a strange land, language, religion and customs. It is purely from the empowerment of this spirit that the people of the African Diaspora have been able to survive such diverse and relentless forms of hostility over the centuries.

6) 'Sorrow'

The curse of four hundred years has been a long and hard road of affliction, a legacy of bitterness, loss and regret. Some memories are too painful to remember and it can take generations to transcend them.

7) 'The Return-Pursuance of Liberation'

'Hope' is the beginning of a new life, and living is the path to joy. The indomitable spirit leads a disinherited people to a new plain, a new plateau – a chance and moment to reconvene. The hope is to return to the old reality before the rupture and painful separation.

In order of appearance the Multiple Occupancies Collective comprises Jayne O. Ifekwunigwe, Shanti Thomas, Lorraine Ayensu, Folake Shoga and Tunde Jegede. In December 1996 Margaret Boushel of the School for Policy Studies, University of Bristol made an important contribution to our strand as part of the 'Frontlines/Back Yards' conference. The focus of her presentation was 'Vulnerable Multi-Racial Families and Child Welfare Policies'.

CHOOSE YOUR PERSONALITY

Plashet School Drama Group

Plashet School in Plaistow is a girls' school with a majority of Bangladeshi students. The school enjoys the support of its local Asian communities and has developed a vigorous and reflexive style of multiculturalism which encourages students to look critically at issues of race, ethnicity and national identification.

Students from Plashet School.

The Head of Drama, Sue Rosner, working with an artist in residence, devised a drama project with a group of Year 10 students, using some of the conference themes to explore, through improvisation, issues of identity and difference. The piece is built around a spoof of Blind Date, called Choose Your Personality. The extract below is from the final scene.

Soomia: Last week we had a big trauma with Choosing Your Personality, so let's have a quick reminder of what went on. On last week's show Melissa changed all the rules. She not only turned down two personalities, she turned down all THREE! So now let's welcome Melissa.

So why did you come on Choosing Your Personality last week?
Nasrin: I was just really confused. People were always telling me what to do.
Soomia: Well wasn't that the whole point of coming on 'Choose Your Personality' – to choose one!
Nasrin: I just realised that I didn't want to decide between the choices I had been given. I should be able to do what I want.
Soomia: So you said you wanted to be yourself. How long do you think you'd be able to keep that up?
Nasrin: Forever. I would try to keep it up forever, because I would be doing what I want.
Soomia: All right. Thank you for coming on the show. Next week, let's hope we don't have Michael doing the same thing.
Nasrin: My sister hates the way I dress, so she wanted me to choose Personality Number 1, because she was fashionable. My Mum, she doesn't want me to do anything that I'll regret in the future, so she wanted me to choose Number 2, who always follows advice. My friends wanted me to go out with them all the time, so they wanted me to choose Number 3 – the raver. But I'm not like any of these personalities. People should accept me for what I am, and not try to change me. We are young, we live in a multicultural society, and most importantly we're individuals – so accept us for what we are, and don't judge us by the way we look.

As part of their preparation for the improvised drama the group explored a number of key words related to the conference theme. They took some of the definitions from dictionaries and added some of their own (indicated in italics):

TRADITION The action of handing over; that which is handed down or transmitted from generation to generation by word of mouth; a long-established and accepted custom; among the Jews part of an unwritten code received from Moses, and passed on in the Misnah; among the Christians, the recorded sayings and teachings of Christ and the apostles and the communications of the Holy Spirit which have equal authority with the scriptures; among the Moslems an account of the sayings and doings of Mohammed, transmitted first by word of mouth and then written down; a giving up, surrender or betrayal; the surrender of sacred books in a time of persecution; *what elders refer to when they want young people to do what they're told and follow their example.*

MODERN Originating in the current age; the better-known living literary languages of Europe (sometimes just French and German);

subjects of school instruction which are not ancient; not antiquated or obsolete; everyday, ordinary or commonplace; *youth*.

FUNDAMENTAL The foundation, basis or groundwork; a leading or primary principle, rule or law; the lowest or root note of a chord.

HUMAN Secular (not religious?); characteristic of man (not woman?); civil, courteous, obliging, benevolent; *someone who is kind to animals, women and the elderly*.

RACE Offspring; a set of children or descendants; a generation, a house, lineage or tribe; a nation or people of common stock; one of the great divisions of mankind having certain common physical or moral characteristics; a natural or inherited disposition of a particular people or ethnic group.

ETHNIC Gentile; heathen; pagan; pertaining to the customs, habits and beliefs of nations or peoples; pertaining to nations which are not Christian or Jewish; *what white people call us because we're different from them; where people say they are coming from, when they are trying to work out where they are going.*

ETHNOMANIAC *Someone who is crazy about roots.*

ABSOLUTE Detached; disengaged; perfect; complete; entire; unconditional; existing without relation to any other being; *lonely*.

SEGREGATION TOMORROW

Bill Schwarz

If the twentieth century has been the century of the colour-line, then May 1954 marks a critical turning point. On 7 May, after a siege of eight weeks, the French were vanquished at Dien Bien Phu. This was the first moment in history when an insurgent guerrilla army defeated a colonial power and expelled it from its lands. It made possible the Bandung Conference of the following year, and also made plausible its rhetoric proclaiming the end of the epoch of the white man. The defeat at Dien Bien Phu did much to induce in the French army a psychotic vengefulness against non-white peoples, which later was to dominate the war in Algeria – and which was to enter 'theory' in our own postcolonial times through the writings of Frantz Fanon. In the aftermath of this spectacular collapse of French power in Vietnam, the USA was inexorably drawn into the vacuum. On five separate occasions in 1954 Eisenhower was advised by his National Security Council, abetted by John Foster Dulles and Vice-President Richard Nixon, once more to unleash atomic bombs on hostile Asian countries.[1]

1. Stephen E. Ambrose, *Eisenhower. Vol.II. The president, 1952-69*, Allen and Unwin, London 1984, p229.

Ten days after Dien Bien Phu the US Supreme Court, in its ruling on *Brown v the Board of Education*, outlawed segregation in the nation's schools, a decision that created momentary jubilation amongst blacks in every corner of the nation.

These two events, one domestic to the USA, the other more obviously international in its ramifications, dramatically repositioned the frontlines of race in the US, triggering a tectonic shift that reordered the foundations of American civilization. This transformation, slow in its early moments in the 1950s but accelerating wildly in the 1960s, polarized America. By the time of Black Power in the mid-1960s, 'Vietnam' and 'race' no longer appeared as separate issues: increasingly they marked a public frontline, dividing the official nation from its myriad of malcontents.

The Supreme Court ruling produced its own white backlash. White supremacy had been built into the civic structures of life in the South: palpable, unassailable, terrifying. In the twentieth century it had never become, for long, a manifest political issue in the Southern states, for white voters had never been in much dispute about its founding principles, and blacks had been violently excluded from the institutions of citizenship. Faith in white supremacy was what politics was, and it required neither discussion nor debate. Federal intervention, in *Brown v Board of Education*, turned this around. For whites in the South, *Brown* codified their new social role as victim. Segregation became a political issue, and those who upheld its continued existence increasingly found themselves, in public at least, having to invent a putatively democratic and universal language – in which race barely dared to speak its name – in order to maintain their own supremacy.

We can see this, for example, in the political career of George Wallace, the future governor of Alabama. As a true son of a remembered Confederate past, he was born and bred a common-or-garden white supremacist. Yet in the late 1940s, when he first became involved in politics, he only hesitantly allied himself to the political banner of white supremacy: he was instinctively a Southern Roosevelt Democrat, making the distinctive populism of the South his own. Wallace discovered, however, that the backwoods world of the South in which he had grown up was on the point of dramatic dislocation, and that the indigenous white citizens of his state, on whom he depended for political advancement, were not at all inhibited about turning race into the axiomatic political issue; nor were they squeamish about bringing into the public sphere the seemingly uneventful racist vernacular of daily life. Events, however, passed Wallace by. The Klan had already re-emerged as a significant force in Alabama in the immediate postwar years.[2] Wallace saw the state governor, his own political mentor Big Jim Folsom, humiliated for being soft on race. In the immediate aftermath of *Brown v Board of Education* the white backlash assumed an organized public form, spreading from Mississippi across the Southern states, cohering around a variety of well-funded Citizens' Councils. Wallace listened to these shifts in the popular mood. After the *Brown* ruling he drew away from Folsom, yet even so, in his first gubernatorial campaign in 1958 he was defeated, largely due to the perception that he, too, was insufficiently attuned to the imperatives of white supremacy – a by-way in the twentieth-century history of the colour-line that takes some comprehending. The 1958 campaign stiffened his resolve. Wallace had been born a robust, regular racist: but in 1958, as a genuine populist, he had begun to realize that he needed to learn *the politics* of race.

The next election for governor, he won. On 14 January 1963, on a freezing day in Montgomery, he delivered his inaugural speech. Those listening to him donned white flowers to signify their allegiance to Anglo-Saxon supremacy. Wallace's speech had been drafted by former Klansman Asa Carter. It played on the memories of the Civil War, not as some distant historic event, but as an imaginative act of the present. It played too on fears of beleaguered white minorities in distant lands: 'The Belgian survivors of the Congo cannot present their case to the United Nations ... nor [can] the citizens of Oxford, Mississippi'. White Southerners were, Wallace declared, nothing less than an oppressed people, their commitment to white supremacy notwithstanding. A new politics was required – heroic, on the one hand, but driven by the will of the poor and the oppressed on the other – in order to turn the world the right way up again. In this task Alabama could call upon a providential history, for in

2. Glenn Feldman, 'Soft opposition. Elite acquiescence and Klan-sponsored terrorism in Alabama, 1946-50', *Historical Journal* 40:3, 1997.

3. Dan T. Carter, *The Politics of Rage. George Wallace, the origins of the new conservatism, and the transformation of American politics*, Simon and Schuster, New York 1995, p11.

4. Powell visited the USA on a single occasion, in October 1967. He expressed his own fears to an American visitor shortly after his return to London: 'Integration of races of totally disparate origins and culture is one of the great myths of our time. It has never worked throughout history. The United States lost its only real opportunity of solving its racial problem when it failed after the Civil War to partition the old Confederacy into a 'South Africa' and a 'Liberia', Andrew Roth, *Enoch Powell: Tory tribune*, Macdonald, London 1970, p341.

5. For a suitably hair-raising account of the response of the Los Angeles Police Department, and of its infamous Chief, William Parker, see Mike Davis, *City of Quartz. Excavating the future in Los Angeles*, Vintage, London 1970, p341.

6. One of the best examples is Ronald Segal, *The Race War*, Bantam Books, New York 1967, which takes a global view.

Montgomery was to be found 'this very heart of the Great Anglo-Saxon Southland'. And Wallace himself was to embody this intransigence: 'I draw the line in the dust and toss the gauntlet before the feet of tyranny... and I say ... segregation now ... segregation tomorrow ... segregation forever'.[3]

Through the 1960s Wallace, and others like him, made many such declarations, not only in the USA, but also in the metropolitan heartlands of a decaying European colonialism. Theirs was a powerful voice in the orchestration of that 'Other '68' – the '68 of the radical right. At the end of the century the historical consequences of this neo-conservatism, which had been founded in the 1960s, are all too evident. They have entered the deepest reflexes of our own political lives, constraining what can be imagined and disorganizing the utopian, libertarian impulse of the *hoi-polloi* '68 – that '68 which Wallace himself did much to break. In the 1990s, we are now living, a generation later, in his 'tomorrow'. Yet for all the evident advances of the new conservatism in the intervening years, any established public figure advocating in our own times 'segregation forever' – in the old idiom – would bring about their own immediate political oblivion. Indeed the dystopian projections summoned by the likes of Wallace in North America, or Enoch Powell in Britain – in which ethnic mixing is the norm, in which black and white make love, and in which there appears a new generation of 'coffee-coloured' children – have not only happened, but now pass as the common currency of a postmodern media culture. In confronting the politics of race in our own day there is still plenty which can chill the blood. But we need to recall what *has* changed.

Nor should we forget, to continue this theme, that 'the race war' which was predicted from many different quarters through the 1960s never did in fact break out. From the urban conflagration of Watts in 1965, through the riots of Newark and Detroit in the two years which followed, there emerged terrifying predictions of all-out warfare between black and white. Though these fears were triggered by events in the US, they had considerably greater reach: the racial fear witnessed by Enoch Powell in the States, for example, directly influenced his determination to 'speak out' on race a few months later in Birmingham, England.[4] Some of these predictions were simply part and parcel of the larger *grand peur* which gripped the white imagination after Watts. Yet they could also prove to be dangerously self-fulfilling. The colossal militarization of urban police forces throughout the USA in these years signalled more clearly than anything the belief that, when it came to the defence of white privilege, no quarter would be given.[5] Other voices were less febrile, recognizing precisely that white privilege was the issue, and suggesting that if no accommodation were made, Armageddon would ensue.[6]

To reflect on recent history in this way, and to try to get some perspective on how the racially segregated worlds of the 1950s have been transformed into habitats less fearful, with greater ease of mutual transaction, does not mean as a corollary that all has been benign.[7] Even if the anticipated Manichean onslaught between black and white never occurred, ethnocide has happened – if most frequently at some remove from the old power-centres of the imperial system. The local contours of many front-lines can still be steeped in terror, both symbolic and real. And faith in the necessity for ethnic purity is present in fifty-seven different varieties.

It is both the unevenness and the opaqueness of these transformations which are at issue, the metaphor of frontline only partially capturing the complexities in the dispositions of power. For this was a realignment which turned on the dismantling of legal segregation – yet which at the same time drove *race* to the centre of national politics. This is the defining paradox of the racial politics of the period. If in the US the civil rights movement of the mid-1950s to the mid-1960s were the principal agent in the realization of the former, George Wallace can be credited as having been a prime mover in the organization of the latter.

My own interest in these issues arises from the British experience. On the back of white resistance to black immigration, Enoch Powell forced race on to the agenda of public life while all the while proclaiming, in startled exasperation, that his own hands were clean. As others have persuasively argued, it was along this axis of race that the postwar settlement disintegrated and a new authoritarianism cohered. So profoundly encoded was this authoritarianism in the symbolic repertoire of race that their organizing signifiers came to be interchangeable, such that appeals to general virtues – to ethics, law, order, prosperity – at the same time surreptitiously worked as appeals to racial fear.[8] Coming late in the day to the US experience I was struck, for all the differences, by the symmetry of the trajectories of racial politics in the USA and the UK. In quite different political conjunctures race came to define the national political agenda, but (with some notable exceptions) did this most effectively when it remained coded. It was a presence everyone knew to be there: unspeakable, but incapable of remaining unspoken.

To turn from the political culture of the English to that of the USA is like entering the familiar *mise-en-scene* of a noir-ish B-movie. The culture of Westminster is highly centralized. And it is steeped in the conviction of its own *civility*. The localism of North American politics creates a system which is a deal more elastic, allowing greater scope for local bosses, hucksters and *caudillos* to get nearer to the centre of things – some of whom, on occasion, make it to the White House and take their entourage from back home with them. This localism has also meant that the modernization of US politics has been strikingly uneven. To read of Lyndon Johnson in the 1930s sending out pick-ups to transfer ballot-papers from one county to the next, or of Wallace getting kick-backs from selling asphalt to his own highway programme in the 1960s, is to be confronted by all the theatricality of a Burbank hoodlum: it makes sleaze, in the British style, look merely quaint.

7. Henry Louis Gates, *Coloured People*, Penguin, Harmondsworth 1995, provides a moving, if ambivalent, memoir.

8. Stuart Hall *et al.*, *Policing The Crisis. Mugging, the state and law and order*, Macmillan, London 1978.

But this is also a political culture – in contrast to the British – which generates critical commentaries which are both literate and well-researched, and (in so far as all these things are relative) popular. 'Only a reckless verisimilitude can set the line straight', announces James Ellroy in the preface to *American Tabloid*, the novel which carries his ferocious indictment of the Kennedys; and it is this conviction which provides the rationale for the epic of sadism and pathological possessive individualism which follows. This is a viewpoint as far removed from the genteel biographies of British politicians – which attest to the unfailing saintliness and perspicacity of generations of dutiful individuals, noticing only the littlest of human foibles – as one can possibly imagine.

The recklessness of James Ellroy's verisimilitude lies in his relentless, anarchic, Sorelian vision of public life in America, a mode of writing which inverts the gentility of the hagiography. Its popularity, one might deduce, derives from the commonsense belief that all politicians are bastards. His is a visceral prose. It's not devoid of insight – though it soon palls, its very recklessness all-too-quickly becoming predictable. Other, less desperate, encounters carry us further. One fine, recent example, is Dan T. Carter's study of George Wallace and of his place in the neo-conservative offensive of the 1960s, from which I've drawn here. It contains many illuminating arguments. I wish to focus on only one: on the connections he makes between race and the realignment of national politics.[9]

9. Carter, *op.cit.*; and for the historiographical context, Michael Kazin, 'The grass-roots right. New histories of US conservatism in the twentieth century', *American Historical Review* 97:1, 1992. All my information on Wallace I take from Carter; indeed, this goes for some of his central arguments too. All I attempt here is to think through the parallel trajectories in the USA and Britain.

On four occasions Wallace mounted a campaign for the presidency: in 1964, 1968, 1972, and – even after he was severely crippled following the assassination attempt on 15 May 1972 – again in 1976. The common characteristic in each of his campaigns was his wildcat populism which, on the one hand, kept him constant on the theme of white victimization while, on the other, sent him spinning in relation to the established party institutions. For good reason he could never decide where his allegiances should rest. His inherited loyalties pulled him to the Democrats. His sympathies took him to the Republicans, especially after first Goldwater, and then Nixon, made the running. And desperation and frustration – combined, it has to be said, with a measure of cool strategic calculation – had him inventing all manner of third-party machinations, made up, as even he came to admit, of the full gamut of kooks and cranks. In terms of the given political landscape one never knew where he would be next. Despite all the fire and brimstone, and despite many local electoral advances, each campaign burnt him up, as if every victory brought his own destruction nearer – which in a sense it did. For the electoral system, as much as for any outsider, was stacked against him.

But politics, in the larger sense, is only minimally about elections. On four occasions, Wallace self-destructed electorally, but ultimately could claim that he had shaped at least one party – the Republicans – in his own image, and maybe too, in a deeper sense, the federal state. In moving from his natal incarnation as a New Deal Democrat to being the 'alchemist', as

Dan Carter suggests, of the new conservatism – personified in its earliest stages by Nixon – Wallace was the archetype of the conservative militant of the 1960s.[10]

10. Carter, *op.cit*, p12.

From one perspective – of poor white Alabama – this was no transformation at all. The New Deal spoke the language, dear to the founding myths of the nation, of the little man confronted, as Roosevelt put it in his second inaugural, by 'blind economic forces and blindly selfish men'; whereas Wallace in the 1960s spoke out against the tyranny of big government, against the vested interests of federal politicians, judges and bureaucrats, against the media and, most virulently, against those liberal whites wealthy enough to buy themselves out of the social consequences of desegregation – out of, as it were, 'race' itself.

This was a populism which turned on race, but which was articulated in terms of an external enemy bent on the destruction of the 'way of life' of historic Alabama. When Wallace ran for governor in 1962 he declared he would defend the rights of Alabama as a 'sovereign state' – 'even to the point of standing at the schoolhouse door' – while denouncing his opponents, looking to compromise or capitulate on the issue of segregation, as 'sissy britches'. As governor, in June 1963, he made his stand. Wallace, in a carefully orchestrated media-event, barred the entry of federal officials accompanying black students intending to enrol at the University of Alabama. At the end of his oratorical declaration, in which he determined to preserve the integrity of the state and 'the freedoms of the citizens thereof' – and when the newsmen began packing up their cameras – the students, who had previously enrolled elsewhere on the campus, were quietly escorted to their dorms and the drama ended. Integration continued, while the principled intransigence of Governor Wallace appeared, to his loyalists, to remain unsullied. He was to repeat on many occasions that the fundamental confrontation had had nothing to do with race: it was, he insisted, merely a matter of his safeguarding the rights of his people against the incursions of the federal state.[11]

11. *ibid.*, pp105-6, and 149.

As in many such populisms, rhetorical sallies of this type required much vacillation and ambivalence, and much subterfuge. The subterfuge was clear enough to his many detractors. Here was a public figure who controlled a highly militarized, highly effective state machine in order to protect the institutions of white supremacy, and who, in political terms, was far removed from the backwoods, two-dime, honest-to-god image that he projected. The ambivalence derived from his determination to speak both to his white constituency in Alabama and to the nation at large. It is this ambivalence which makes him of interest. He was not simply an eccentric recidivist (as the *New York Times* believed for too long), speaking for a white population whom a putatively providential history had sold down the river, but a figure with the capacity to transform this apparently local mentality into the raw material for a national politics. Wallace was an authentic populist who was driven by authentic electoral ambition. The zig-zags of his public career represent not just indecisiveness, but genuine strategic dilemmas – indicative of a man who both wanted radically to refashion the political world, and who wanted it to deliver him office. These zigs-zags represent his need both to be seen as the premier public representative of white America and as a credible national figure who had left his backyard racism far behind.

What made this possible was precisely the legislative victories of the civil rights movement, carried into statute by Kennedy and Johnson. Neither of the Kennedy brothers was much persuaded by the political merits of the civil rights movement. They recognized an ethical legitimacy, but politically they tended to see the black leaders, and the defenders of white supremacy, as two warring factions, representing merely sectional interests, each confirming the backwardness of the South. And they were constantly reminded that their own fortunes depended upon the machine politics of the Southern Democrats in the South. The price they had to pay for this, as they complained often enough, was having to put up with strutting local party bosses in shiny suits. Johnson did not share these sensibilities: consorting with the Democrat tribunes of the South was fine by him, as long as they did his bidding, and the dirtier the deal the better. The last thing expected of him was generosity to any movement which couldn't be controlled by Washington, least of all civil rights. As a congressman for eleven years, he had voted against every civil rights bill that had come his way. Even so Kennedy, on the night of Wallace's defence of 'the schoolhouse door', made an impromptu decision to announce on television new civil rights legislation, with a view to ending segregation in private as well as public facilities. A year later Johnson signed the bill. And on 15 March 1965 – right in the midst of the Selma to Montgomery march and the drama of Edmund Pettus bridge – Lyndon Johnson addressed a special joint session of Congress to declare his own determination to push through, at breakneck speed, the Voting Rights Bill. When, in the course of the televised speech, he uttered the words – 'and we shall over-come' – Wallace was convinced in his own mind that the Democrats and the federal government had unambivalently crossed over to the enemy, selling out the little people of the white South to the liberal nostrums of integration. What better moment than to summon a history ordained by providence?[12]

In the South Wallace could attack the new legislation as an affront to whites, which jeopardized the 'safety of our wives and children'.[13] On the national political stage, he could shift the grounds of his attack by condemning civil rights legislation as exemplifying a liberal state determined to intervene into every corner of civic and family life, seeking to impose bureaucratically contrived blueprints for equality. In this lay the identifiable beginnings of the 'new' conservatism.

Two early episodes demonstrated Wallace's capacity to reach beyond his home constituency. The first occurred in June 1963 when, as a poten-

12. For a brilliant account see Robert A. Caro, *The Years of Lyndon Johnson. Vol.II. Means of ascent*, Pimlico, London 1992, ppxiii-xxi.

13. Carter, *op.cit.*, p138.

tial presidential runner, he was invited on to television's most important current affairs programme, *Meet the Press*. He was anxious beforehand that he had nothing to say about foreign policy, and he had worked himself up into a highly nervous state. As it turned out, he delivered a relaxed, reassured performance, all bonhomie and indignant innocence. Not once was foreign policy raised. All the questions were about race. He defended 'separate' development in the South as representing the wishes of both black and white, and he hit the interviewers hard on the issue of racial injustices in the North. In part, Wallace was learning his political lessons – in particular, how to articulate for a wider public his own home-truths. But in part also, he made the discovery that the rhetoric of national politics was coming his way: it was all about race. And here, for audiences who did not know the South, he played his trump. As much as any colonial administrator or white settler from the European empires, he prided himself on the fact that he *knew* the native. 'I don't need a foreign policy', he confessed in private afterwards: 'all they wanted to know about was niggers, and I'm the expert'.[14]

14. *ibid.*, p359.

In the autumn which followed, Wallace toured the Ivy League universities, joking, taunting and demagogic. He wove together his usual condemnation of civil rights legislation with a new emphasis on low taxes and on rolling back state expenditure. In the new year he opened his presidential campaign in Wisconsin. The breakthrough – the second episode – occurred on 1 April. Booked by an ex-marine and bar-owner, Bronko Gruber, to speak at the Serb Memorial Hall in Milwaukee, Wallace faced an audience of 'ethnics' (to employ the psephological jargon of the time), consisting of Serbs, Poles and Hungarians. As he entered, the audience, in a bizarre twist, sang 'Dixie' in English and in a variety of central European languages. Wallace's fierce defence of a god-fearing America, in conjunction with his equally fierce denunciation of civil rights – meaning, in this context, nothing other than *black* – proved for him an intoxicating success. The dominating motifs of a Southern populism had crossed the Mason-Dixie line, in a manner no one could have predicted. Shortly after, in the Indiana and Maryland primaries, Wallace stormed ahead.

In all this, it was never certain to Wallace where exactly he was positioned in terms of party politics. His first moves to enter the presidential race of 1964 had received the backing of wealthy Southern conservatives who had welcomed the idea of him running as an independent. He fought the primaries as a Democrat, though reserving his most corrosive onslaughts for Johnson and the established Democratic leadership. And in July he tried to persuade Goldwater to adopt him as his running-mate, on a Republican ticket. One thing, though, was sure. He had severed the historic connection between white Southerners and the Democratic establishment, easing their migration to the Republicans.

The populist adventurism required to effect this political realignment repeatedly led him down many dead-ends. The most spectacular occurred when he was again running for the presidency in 1968. Formally, he was standing as a candidate for the American Independent Party. In need of a vice-president he canvassed J. Edgar Hoover, Colonel Sanders (the same), and the former Chief of Staff of the Air Force, Curtis LeMay. LeMay, a North American version of Bomber Harris, accepted. In his first press conference he dilated on the virtues of nuclear warfare, expressing his bewilderment at the 'phobia' of Americans toward the bomb. He informed his audience that the ecosystem of Bikini Atoll was flourishing (he had seen a movie about it), though nonetheless he was compelled to concede that some of the crustaceans might still, after some twenty nuclear tests, be 'a little bit hot'. For once, Wallace was silenced.[15]

15. *ibid.*, p375.

Such incidents hardly helped Wallace look a serious contender. But more damaging, in 1968, was the fear amongst segregationists that a vote for Wallace would split the right, and have the effect of letting Hubert Humphrey slip through and win. Nixon wanted Wallace voters; he didn't want Wallace.

By the mid-1960s the heroic days of civil rights – Christian non-violence, freedom rides, the pilgrimages to the South – had come to an end, effectively signalled by the march over Edmund Pettus bridge. King moved his forces to Chicago, where black immiseration was as much the issue as codified segregation. Watts erupted. And Black Power came into being. 'Race' had ceased to be a peculiarly Southern phenomenon. On 6 October 1969 *Newsweek* devoted almost its entire issue to 'The troubled American. A special report on the white majority'. According to the report, half of all white Americans blamed black unemployment on laziness; two-thirds identified blacks with street crime; three-quarters opposed any further integration in schools; 90 per cent opposed any further integration in their neighbourhoods; and 98 per cent opposed busing.[16] This wasn't, quite, the old racism of the South; 'segregation forever' was not the principal logic at work. In views such as these, blackness was perceived as a social problem, threatening the white suburbs; it was a police problem, threatening the stability of neighbourhood and nation; and blacks themselves were largely to blame for their own misfortunes. Blackness desegregated potentially was more *present* – it was both more proximate and more disturbing than hitherto. As Dan Carter argues, this is where an erstwhile liberalism – in the name of hard-headed realism – could imperceptibly transmute into neo-conservatism.

16. *ibid.*, p402.

The main beneficiary of this neo-conservatism was Richard Nixon. Republican strategists, in 1968, fell upon the key idea of 'who hates whom?', and organized an electoral politics accordingly. In this, in North and South alike, fear of what blacks had now become was the dominating motif, and white Southern Democrats were at least potentially the determining constituency. The radicalism of this new conservatism derived from the fact that its high command not only understood that American society would polarize as a result of the measures they advocated, but also that such polarization was actively to be sought, as a virtue in itself. In purely arithmetical terms, John Mitchell was convinced in 1968, the Republicans could win the majority by adopting such a strategy. By and large this was a political frontline which divided the economically independent from the economically hapless, a frontline which was driven, in its innermost symbolism, by unadorned racial fear.

The populist current of this new conservatism ran to the very centre of political life. After his first presidential victory Nixon – whilst reading Robert Blake's *Disraeli* – hoped he would be sufficiently powerful to break out of the two-party system and reorder the political terrain. In July 1970, while president, he first considered the possibility of ditching the Republican label and launching a new 'Conservative Party', composed precisely of Republicans and dissident, neo-conservative, Wallace-influenced Democrats from the South. Recruiting the Texan Democrat, John Connolly, as his Secretary of Treasury in February 1971 and persuading him, the following year, to organize the pressure-group 'Democrats for Nixon', were important initiatives – if not in renaming the Republican Party – at the very least in giving it a new complexion. This was a clear recomposition of the state to the right, notwithstanding Nixon's protestations that he was inventing a new centre-ground of American politics. These hopes of consolidating the array of neo-conservative forces into a new political coalition coincided with Nixon's determination to address 'the forgotten minorities' of the United States. With clear echoes of the politics of the Serb Memorial Hall, he imagined an America polarized between, on the one hand, 'Italians, Poles, Elks and Rotarians' and, on the other, 'Jews, blacks, youth'. This was but a step away – or, in stricter chronology, a matter of weeks – from Nixon's discovery of 'the silent majority'.[17]

Critically, Nixon gave this politics a Southern spin, the legacy of Wallace indelibly present. His Chief of Staff, Bob Haldeman, recorded a classically Nixonite monologue delivered, in private, on the eve of his second presidential election:

> He then got into his feeling for the South, that because of going to school there he had a close feeling and they always resent being put down by the Northerners. Makes the point that union leaders are like the South. They want to abide by the law and they respect the Presidency. He then said the theme to development is in regard to the heartland. Our New American Majority appeals across the board for the same reasons to people. The basic American values. A strong United States patriotism, strong moral and spiritual values. Anti-permissiveness. They are turned off on welfare because it's wrong and because they are anti-elitist, plus they have selfish motives. They are American to the core. The Southerners are more so than the rest of the United States, because they are not poisoned by the elite universities and the

17. H.R. Haldeman, *The Haldeman Diaries. Inside the Nixon White House*, Berkeley Books, New York 1995, pp212, 217, 218, and 242.

media, but we're also high in Polish, Italian, mountain areas, farm states. Weak in the suburbia/big cities because here people are soft. The people that are for permissiveness, anti-United States, and so forth. That square America is coming back and that we didn't just gather a bunch of haters. The real issue is patriotism, morality, religion.[18]

18. *ibid.*, pp631-2.

In such feverish musings what Dan Carter calls the 'Southernization' of US politics – in the South is to be found the true America – received its presidential imprimatur.

That Nixon should move so closely onto his political terrain was bad news for Wallace. Pat Buchanan warned Nixon in the early stages of the 1972 election that if Wallace, as an independent, were not destroyed he would threaten to take some seven million votes from the Republicans while attracting less than half that from the Democrats. Nixon was already on the job. While expressing public sympathy for Wallace, he secretly funded his rivals in Alabama and set the Internal Revenue Service onto both him and his brother. Wallace's decision to return to the Democratic fold, announced in January 1972, coincided with the end of the IRS investigation.

In May Wallace was shot. Nixon and his Special Counsel, Chuck Colson, immediately tried to implicate the assassin as a McGovern loyalist. This was but a prelude to Watergate – to Gordon Liddy, Jeb Magruder and the slow march, as Haldeman for one discovered, to Lampoc Federal Prison. All derived from the wish to neutralize the enemies of the silent majority – and to be sure that the ostensible patriots voted for the newly Southernized Republican president. When Nixon went to visit Wallace in hospital, journalists noticed that, on his arrival, he was already made up in preparation for the TV cameras: the passing of the mantle of leadership of white America, inevitably, was to be a television event.

This, in summary form, is the story Dan Carter tells of Wallace and of the realignment of US politics in the 1960s and 1970s. It shows how a right-wing populism, coming directly out of the white backlash, reworked what politics *was*, and constituted the very foundations of the conservative revival of the 1970s and 1980s.

Despite the different historical circumstances the structural parallels with the British experience are compelling. Indeed, it is precisely the difference in respective circumstances that makes the parallel so extraordinary: in historical formations so *unlike* a common process of neo-conservative recomposition can be identified. Powell was not Wallace, Wolverhampton was not Montgomery, nor were the Race Relations Acts equivalent to the civil rights legislation. While Wallace's political rhetoric, to take the most obvious manifestation of respective national contrasts, embodied the sensibilities of a bare-knuckle Southern prize-fighter, Powell – when not dropping into Urdu – spoke in the idiom of the Third Marquess of Salisbury, with a discernible Brummagem twang. There is a tradition in Britain of right-wing popular movements being organized by toffs. Whatever else, Wallace was no toff.

One can argue, however, that long-time Democratic and Labour voters were disconnected from their traditional affiliations, and what made this happen was – in shorthand – race. The mediums, in each case, were Wallace and Powell. The turning-point, in both the US and the UK, was the moment when the state intervened legislatively to protect the interests of the black minorities. This generated its own populist backlash, which – discursively at least – moved to the very centre of the political life. In each case this produced a period of relative electoral volatility, which in turn was followed by the Republicans and the Conservatives reinventing themselves as the respectable incarnations of a politics which, initially, had been dubbed by the arbiters of public opinion an outrage.

To think of a political culture at this level of abstraction can, at best, be sketchy. More concretely, as a way of concluding, one might suggest that the historical comparison with North America provides a way of thinking about contemporary Britain. There is a genuine difficulty in understanding the contradictory legacies of the racial or ethnic politics of the 1960s and 1970s. It's perfectly feasible to suggest that the inheritances of white supremacy are still powerful; that backyard racism is still as prevalent and as potentially terrifying as ever; and that frontline public life in Britain is still organized around an unspoken faith in the unconscious absolutes of white England. It's equally feasible to suggest that the segregated worlds of the colour-bar have become a deal more free; that what was once the virtual universal repudiation of miscegenation has unravelled; and that the very dynamics of black culture themselves have turned what previously was denigrated into something to be admired, from which white cultures can learn. Both can be true, in different moments, in the same culture.

To understand the simultaneity of these cultural moments requires a degree of conceptual sophistication and openness, and there is much evidence that this work is proceeding. But it is also in part a historical problem, turning on what was and was not spoken in the defining conjuncture of the late 1960s and the early 1970s. Kobena Mercer made this same point some years ago, and the new information on George Wallace confirms his initial insights.[19] We need to go back to 'the other 68' in order to decode the public discourses on race and ethnicity in our own times. For this was the moment, after Wallace and after Powell, that race moved to the centre of things while all the while denying its own presence. It is this essential ambivalence which is still present in public discourse today. Wallace and Powell destroyed themselves politically by determining to speak the unspeakable and by positioning themselves as the Jacobins of newly-subjugated whites. The representatives of the Republican and Conservative parties, in each case, involved themselves in complicated manoeuvres both to be seen to accommodate and to repudiate the new racial militancy of the right, while their own established political worlds

19. On Powell's invention of a *legitimate* language of race, which touches on many of the themes discussed here, see Kobena Mercer, ' "1968". Periodizing politics and identity' in Lawrence Grossberg et al. (eds), *Cultural Studies*, Routledge, London 1992.

were being pulled inexorably into its very force-field. Yet it isn't even as if the racial discourse of Powell, or of Wallace in the USA, was unguarded. One can see them learning to articulate a new politics of race in which the unspeakable could find its voice in the established public sphere. Each of them expended prodigious effort in drawing a line between racism and what they insisted was their duty to speak the truth of race. Those who followed were yet more circumspect, such that race was everywhere and nowhere. Many new masquerades of whiteness, as Kobena Mercer suggests, were spun in these critical years, and which are still present in our own public cultures. To go back and see that Little Caesar of racial politics, George Wallace, learn his business is also to see something of our own culture in Britain evolving.

RACE, PLURALISM AND THE MEANING OF DIFFERENCE

Kenan Malik

'It's good to be different' might be the motto of our times. The celebration of difference, respect for pluralism, avowal of identity politics – these are regarded as the hallmarks of a progressive, anti-racist outlook. At least in part, the anti-racist embrace of difference is fuelled by a hostility to universalism. For most anti-racists today, the Enlightenment project of pursuing a rational, scientific understanding of the natural and social world, and of deriving certain universal principles from fragmented experience, is not only a fantasy, but a racist fantasy. It is a fantasy because the world is too complex and too heterogeneous to be subsumed under a single totalising theory. It is racist because universalism has become a means of imposing Euro-American ideas of rationality and objectivity on other peoples and of denying the possibility of non-Western viewpoints. For many anti-racists, the intellectual arrogance of universalism has led to the attempt to eliminate not just non-Western thought, but non-Aryan peoples too. The road that began with Enlightenment universalism ended in the Nazi death camps.

I want in this paper to show this to be a naive and dangerous view. Far from establishing a critique of racial thinking, the politics of difference appropriates many of its themes and reproduces the very assumptions upon which racism has historically been based. Most critically, the embrace of difference has undermined the capacity to defend equality. The very title of the final debate at the Frontlines/Backyards conference – 'Equalities and the politics of difference' – expresses the problem. Equality cannot have any meaning in the plural. Equality cannot be relative, with different meanings for different social, cultural or sexual groups. If so it ceases to be equality at all, or rather becomes equality in the way racists used to define it – 'equal but different' – in defending segregation or apartheid. Equality requires a common yardstick, or measure of judgement, not a plurality of meanings.

Richard Rorty has observed that the embrace of diversity and the desire for equality are not easily compatible. For Rorty, those whom he calls 'Enlightenment liberals' face a seemingly unresolvable dilemma in their pursuit of both equality and diversity:

> Their liberalism forces them to call any doubts about human equality a result of irrational bias. Yet their connoisseurship of diversity forces them to realise that most of the globe's inhabitants do not believe in

1. Richard Rorty,
*Objectivity,
Relativism and
Truth*, Cambridge
University Press,
Cambridge 1991,
p207.

equality, that such a belief is a Western eccentricity. Since they think it would be shockingly ethnocentric to say 'So what? We Western liberals do believe in it, and so much the better for us', they are stuck.[1]

Rorty himself, a self-avowed 'postmodern bourgeois liberal', solves the problem by arguing that equality is good for 'us' but not necessarily for 'them'. While few would go as far as this, nonetheless Rorty's relativist vision of equality has become an implicit part of anti-racist theory and practice. The meaning of equality has been rewritten in the cause of diversity. We cannot afford, however, to be so careless with equality, not because it is a concept that 'we Western liberals believe in', but because it is at the heart of any form of emancipatory politics. Abandoning equality means in effect abandoning the possibility of emancipation. The debate between pluralism and universalism is more than simply of theoretical concern; it relates to fundamental issues about political and social change and it is in this context that I want to discuss the meaning of 'difference' in contemporary society.

There are three basic points I want to argue in this paper. First, I want to show that 'difference' has always been at the heart, not of the anti-racist, but of the racist agenda. Second, I want to argue that cultural pluralism, far from being a means to liberate the voice of the oppressed, is rooted in the same philosophy that gave rise to the discourse of race. Finally, I want to show that in a world that is profoundly unequal, the pursuit of difference inevitably leads to the accommodation to, and exacerbation of, such inequalities.

The irony in the contemporary embrace of difference is that antiracist hostility to universalism mirrors that of traditional racial theorists. Nineteenth-century racial thinkers despised what they regarded as the abstract universalism of Enlightenment thinkers which they believed denied, and even undermined, the concrete reality of human differences. In its stead racial theorists embraced the relative and the particular. Dismissing claims of a universal humanity, they advocated instead the notion that human groups are in profound ways distinct and should be treated accordingly.

French historian and racial thinker Hippolyte Taine mocked the Enlightenment belief that 'men of every race and century were all but identical: the Greek, the barbarian, the Hindoo, the man of the Renaissance, and the man of the eighteenth century as if they had been turned out of a common mould, and all in conformity to a certain abstract conception, which served for the human race.' Echoing the jibe of Catholic reactionary Joseph de Maistre that 'I have seen Frenchmen, Italians, Russians, and so on ... but I must say, as for *man*, I have never come across him anywhere', Taine believed that Enlightenment *philosophes* 'knew man, but not men': 'They did not know that the moral constitution of a people or an age is as particular or as distinct as the physical structure of a family of plants or an order of animals.'[2] Or, as the French psychologist and racial scientist

2. Hippolyte Taine,
*History of English
Literature*, Gebbie
Publishing,
Philadelphia,
Pennsylvania 1897
[first pub. 1864],
vol.1, p8.

Gustav LeBon put it, 'the substitution of relative ideas for abstract notions' was 'one of the greatest conquests of science.'[3]

The discourse of race arose out of the degradation of Enlightenment universalism, and in particular the espousal of Romantic notions of difference: the belief that humanity can be divided into discrete groups; that each group should be considered in its own terms; that each is incommensurate with the others; that the important relationships in society arise in some way out of the differences between groups; and that equality is a meaningless abstract term. It developed in response to a central contradiction in post-Enlightenment society: the contradiction between an abstract belief in equality and the reality of unequal society.

Before the modern concept of race could develop, the modern concepts of equality and humanity had to develop too. Racial difference and inequality can only have meaning in a world which has accepted the possibility of social equality and a common humanity. The achievement of the Enlightenment was that it helped produce just such a world. Whatever their other differences most Enlightenment thinkers held that humans were by nature rational and sociable, and that there existed a common human nature. Implicit in these beliefs was the idea that all humans were potentially equal. Through Enlightenment philosophy humanity had for the first time a concept of universality that could transcend perceived differences.

What is striking about Enlightenment discourse is the lack of any discussion of race. Compared to writings both before and after, eighteenth-century writings show a remarkable disdain for racial arguments. When in 1800 the French anthropologist Joseph-Marie Degerando wrote a methodological text for the *Societe des Observateurs de l'Homme*, the principal anthropological society of its time, he did not think it necessary to deal with the question of race.[4] Again, the debate about slavery that raged through the eighteenth century was rarely a debate about race. With one or two notable exceptions, those who defended slavery did so not on racial grounds but as a defence of the sanctity of property.[5]

Of course Enlightenment thinkers clearly held racist views, some very overtly. It would have been astonishing if it had been otherwise. The racial comments of the likes of Kant, Hume and Voltaire are well known.[6] But what was absent at this time was any sustained discourse of race. Michael Banton, Robert Miles and Anthony Barker, in their various surveys of racial thinking, have all argued, in Banton's words, that 'though there was a substantial literature in the seventeenth and eighteenth centuries about Africans and other non-European peoples, the word "race" was rarely used either to describe peoples or in accounts of differences between them.'[7]

The Enlightenment, however, was not simply an intellectual movement. The belief in equality and a common humanity was the ideological embodiment of a wider social and political movement through which the feudal

3. Gustav LeBon, *The Psychology of Peoples*, G. E. Stechert, New York 1912 [first pub. 1894], pp216-217.

4. Joseph-Marie Degerando, *Observation of Savage Peoples*, University of California Press, Berkeley, California 1969 [first pub. 1800].

5. See, for example, Robin Blackburn, *The Overthrow of Colonial Slavery, 1776-1848*, Verso, London 1988; David Brion Davis, *The Problem of Slavery in the Age of Revolution 1770-1823*, Oxford University Press, Oxford 1989; Seymour Drescher, *Capitalism and Antislavery: British mobilisation in comparative perspective*, Oxford University Press, Oxford 1986; Anthony Barker, *The African Link: British attitudes to the negro in the age of the Atlantic slave trade, 1550-1807*, Frank Cass, London 1978.

6. See David Hume, 'Of National Characters', in *Essays, Moral Political and Literary*, Longman, Green and Co, London 1889 [first pub. 1748]; Immanuel Kant, *Observations on the Feeling of the Beautiful and Sublime*, University of California Press, Berkeley, California 1960 [first pub. 1764]; Francois-

Marie Arouet
Voltaire, 'Essays on
the customs and
spirit of the nations',
in *The Age of Louis
XIV and Other
Selected Writings*,
Washington Square
Press, New York
City 1963 [first pub.
1756-75].

7. Michael Banton,
Racial Theories,
Cambridge
University Press,
Cambridge 1987,
pp8-9; Robert Miles,
Racism, Routledge,
London 1989;
Barker, *op.cit.*.

8. 'Wherever there is
great poverty, there
is great inequality.
For every one rich
man there must be at
least five hundred
poor, and the afflu-
ence of the few
supposes the "indi-
gence of the many"',
Adam Smith, *An
Inquiry into the
Nature and Causes
of the Wealth of
Nations*, Oxford
University Press,
Oxford 1993 [first
pub. 1776], p408.

9. For an extended
analysis of the
making of the
discourse of race, see
Kenan Malik, *The
Meaning of Race:
race, history and
culture in Western
society*, Macmillan,
Basingstoke 1996,
esp chs 2-4.

order crumbled and a new society – capitalism – emerged. Out of the complex interaction between the ideology of equality and developing capitalist social relations emerged the discourse of race.

The tolerance, egalitarianism and optimism that characterised the Enlightenment derived, at least in part, from the relative stability of Europe in the first part of the eighteenth century. There existed an almost universal conviction that the social order was static, or at least that change would be orderly and contained. The social upheaval created by the coming of market relations upset such convictions and brought into focus the immanent contradictory attitudes of the bourgeoisie towards the idea of equality. Belief in equality was at the heart of the bourgeois political programme. Yet the pursuit of equality threatened to undermine that very political programme, for, as Adam Smith suggested, the defence of private property seemed to require a defence of inequality.[8]

At the same time the emerging capitalist social relations placed constraints upon the extension of equality. Capitalist ideology expressed hostility to the parochial, irrational nature of feudalism and proclaimed a belief in human equality and a universal society. In practice, however, the particular forms of capitalist society placed limits on the expression of equality. Capitalism destroyed the parochialism of feudal society but it created divisions anew; divisions which, moreover, seemed as permanent as the old feudal ones. As social inequalities persisted in the new society, and acquired the stamp of permanence, so these inequalities began to present themselves as if they were natural, not social.

The discourse of race emerged as a means of reconciling the conflict between the ideology of equality and the reality of the persistence of inequality. From the racial viewpoint, inequality persisted because society was by nature unequal. The destiny of different social groups was shaped, at least in part, by their intrinsic properties. Humanity was divided into discrete groups, each with particular properties, and the divisions between the groups were immutable and unchanging. Racial ideology was the inevitable product of the persistence of differences of rank, class and peoples in a society that had accepted the concept of equality. Race came to be the way through which people made sense of the world around them.[9]

There are two important points here. First, the concept of race was not implicit in Enlightenment categories. It emerged out of the interaction between Enlightenment categories and the social relations of emergent capitalist society. The Enlightenment helped establish for the first time, in theory at least, the possibility of human emancipation. But it did so in social circumstances that limited the expression of its emancipatory potential. Where social forces drawing on the logic of Enlightenment discourse had sufficient strength – as, for instance, in the Haitian Revolution led by Toussaint l'Ouverture – they could pursue the goal of equality beyond that envisaged by those who drew up the Declaration of the Rights of Man, or the American Declaration of Independence. But where such forces were weak, the contradictory attitude of the capitalist class towards equality ensured that increasing limits were placed upon its expression. The narrative of race is thus also the narrative of the containment of the movements for social emancipation.

The second point that emerges from this discussion is that universalism did not give rise to race; rather the discourse of race developed in opposition to the notions of universalism and rationalism. It was through the Romantic reaction to the Enlightenment that racial ideology first found expression. Romantics rejected what they saw as the abstract nature of Enlightenment universalism, and championed instead particularist accounts of human difference. They considered every people to be unique, and that such uniqueness was expressed through its *volksgeist*, the unchanging spirit of a people refined through history. The idea of *volksgeist* became transformed into the concept of racial make-up, an unchanging substance, the foundation of all physical appearance and mental potential and the basis for division and difference within humankind. At the root of modern racism, therefore, lie not Enlightenment concepts of universality but Romantic visions of human differences.

Understanding the historical and intellectual roots of the idea of race is important because Romantic notions of human differences also lie at the heart of contemporary visions of cultural pluralism. Racial theory and cultural pluralism both display a hostility to Enlightenment universalism, but in different ways. Ernest Gellner has pointed out that there are two sets of questions that arise from the debate between universalism and relativism: 'Is there but one kind of man, or are there many? Is there but one world, or are there many?'[10] While the first questions the biological unity of humankind, the second questions the very idea of a single truth or objective understanding of the world.

10. Ernest Gellner, *Relativism and the Social Sciences*, Cambridge University Press 1985, p83.

Belief in a single world assumes that common laws and values operate across all societies but that different people respond in different ways to them. The nineteenth-century social Darwinist, Herbert Spencer, expressed this idea well when he explained how his views differed from those of Enlightenment philosophers:

> In early life we have been taught that human nature is everywhere the same ... This error we must replace by the truth that the laws of thought are everywhere the same.[11]

11. Cited in George Stocking, *Race, Culture and Evolution: essays in the history of anthropology*, University of Chicago Press, Chicago, Illinois 1982, p117.

For Spencer, therefore, the same objective social laws operate in every society and culture, but different peoples respond to these objective laws in different ways, the nature of the response being determined by the racial make-up of any given people.

Belief in many worlds, on the other hand, denies a common objective understanding of the world and in its place posits a plurality of ways of

RACE, PLURALISM AND THE MEANING OF DIFFERENCE   129

understanding and evaluating the world around us. Since the social worlds are not given in nature but constructed by the people who inhabit them, so every world is specific to the people who inhabit it and incommensurate with the social worlds that other people inhabit.

Schematically, one may say that the discourse of race (or more specifically the discourse of scientific racism) holds that there is one world but that it is inhabited by different types of humanity, while the discourse of culture holds that there is one type of humanity, but it inhabits different worlds. Of course the distinction between the two is not a clear-cut or straightforward one. Many racial formalists have also denied the possibility of a single truth, while cultural relativists have often accepted the idea of biological differences within humankind. Nevertheless we can perceive in the last decades of the nineteenth century and the first decades of the twentieth a shift from the discourse of race to the discourse of culture which is largely embodied in a shift from a belief in a single world inhabited by different types of humanity to a belief in a single type of humanity inhabiting different cultural or symbolic worlds.

The discourse of race and the discourse of culture both emerged out of the degradation of universalism, but they did so in different ways. Nineteenth-century racial theorists, for all their disdain of universalist ideas, maintained nevertheless a belief in the idea of reason as a weapon of social transformation and of social progress as the companion of a teleological history. Given this belief in inevitable social progress, the growing gulf between 'civilised man' and the 'primitives' that was evident both within and without European society led many to see such differences in natural, and hence in racial, terms. Victorian social evolutionists were led to posit a hierarchical view of humanity, seeing different groups of peoples as arrested at different points along the evolutionary scale and believing that progress and reason were the prerogative only of certain races.

The discourse of culture, on the other hand, reflected a disenchantment with the notion of social evolution, a disbelief in the doctrine of inevitable social progress and a disillusionment with the values of one's own culture. It was the emergence of such trends in the early part of this century, and in particular in the wake of the First World War which gave rise to relativist theories of culture. In the context of a general pessimism about social progress, the idea of difference was transformed from the notion of 'many men in a single world' to a 'single type of man inhabiting many worlds'. If social development had not overcome the vast gulfs that separated different peoples, many argued, then perhaps that was because such differences reflected the fact that different peoples inhabited different social worlds, each of which was as valid and as real as the other.

The main force in the shift from a racial to a cultural view of human differences was the science of anthropology. Anthropology had always been the most particularist of the human sciences. In the context of Victorian positivism and social evolutionism, this manifested itself through physical anthropology and theories of biological differences. As the positivist outlook disintegrated along with the nineteenth century, so anthropological particularism re-expressed itself in cultural terms.

The central figure in the story of the remaking of anthropology was the German-American Franz Boas. It would be difficult to overestimate the impact of Boas, not simply on anthropology, but on our everyday perceptions of race, culture and difference. Contemporary ideas of pluralism and multiculturalism, of respect for other cultures, and of the importance of tradition and history are all significant themes in Boas' work.[12] His legacy, however, like that of pluralism itself, remains an ambiguous one. Boas, and his students such as Melville Herskovitz, Ruth Benedict and Margaret Mead, played a prominent part in the replacement of racial theories of human differences with cultural theories, and in so doing helped undermine the power of scientific racism. Yet the concept of culture Boas helped develop, to a large extent re-articulated the themes of racial theory in a different guise. Influenced both by the German Romantic tradition and by a liberal egalitarian view, Boas faced the problem, as the historian George Stocking observes, of how to define the Romantic notion of 'the genius of the people' in terms other than racial heredity.[13] His answer, ultimately, was the anthropological concept of culture.

Boas' philosophical egalitarianism and cultural relativism arose from his disillusionment with 'Western' values. He related in a letter the impact of meeting the Inuit on a field trip to the Arctic: 'I often ask myself what advantages our "good society" possesses over that of the "savages". The more I see of their customs the more I realise we have no right to look down on them ... As a thinking person, for me the most important result of this trip lies in the strengthening of my point of view that the idea of a "cultured" person is merely relative.'[14]

Boas' disillusionment was at the root of the ambiguity in his treatment of the idea of equality. The revolutionary egalitarianism that arose out of the Enlightenment was positive and forward-looking. From Condorcet to Marx, such egalitarians held that social progress could overcome artificial divisions and differences and reveal our essential commonality. Boas' egalitarianism arose, on the contrary, from the belief that such progress was not possible. Humanity was equal, not because differences could be overcome, but because every difference was equally valid. But this approach elided 'differences' and 'inequalities'. What were considered differences between individuals and peoples were in reality the product of social inequalities. For Boas, 'equality' meant the acceptance of the actual inequalities of society, but the regarding of these inequalities as different manifestations of a common humanity.

We can see the way in which the new anthropology reframed the meaning of inequality by looking at the development of pluralism in the colonial context. The concept of a plural society first emerged through anthropological analyses of colonial societies in the first decades of this

12. Franz Boas, *The Mind of Primitive Man*, Free Press, New York City 1965 [first pub. 1911]; Melville J. Herskovits, *Franz Boas: the science of man in the making*, American Anthropological Association, Memoir No.89, San Francisco, California 1959.

13. Stocking, *op.cit.*, p214.

14. *ibid.*, p148.

century. In a study of Indonesia and Burma, the anthropologist J.S. Furnivall wrote that 'the first thing that strikes the visitor is the medley of peoples – European, Chinese, Indian and native' that constitute the society. The different groups, Furnivall wrote, 'mix but do not combine'. Each group 'holds by its own religion, its own culture and language, its ideas and ways'. The result was a 'plural society, with different sections of the society living side by side but separately within the same political unit.'[15]

15. J. S. Furnivall, *Colonial Policy and Practice: a comparative study of Burma, Netherlands and India*, New York University Press, New York City 1956, p304.

This concept of a plural society proved attractive both to colonial administrators, grappling with the problem of imposing law and order on the territories, and to Western liberals keen to protect colonial subjects from the ravages of imperialism. Pluralism quickly moved from being a *description* of colonial society to an *explanation* for it. The inequalities of colonial society were rationalised as products of the different cultural outlooks and lifestyles of the various groups that constituted that society. Through this process *inequality* became reframed as *difference*. Like racial theory, plural theory provided an apology for social inequalities, portraying them as the inevitable result, not of natural variations, but of cultural differences.

Pluralism effectively turned on its side the evolutionary ladder of Victorian racial theory: pluralists conceived of humanity as horizontally, rather than vertically, segmented. Humanity was not arranged at different points along an ever-rising vertical axis, as the social evolutionists had believed, but at different points along a stationary horizontal axis. Humanity was composed of a multitude of peoples each inhabiting their own symbolic and cultural worlds. But whether differences were seen as biological or cultural, whether or not they were seen in terms of inferiority and superiority, racial theory and cultural pluralism were characterised by a common hostility to universalism, a disdain for humanism and a philosophical, and occasionally epistemological, relativism.

The consequence of all this can be seen in the debate about race and difference in the postwar world. Following the experience of Nazism, the Holocaust and the Final Solution, biological theories of human differences became discredited. But if racial science was buried in the postwar world, racial thinking was not. While the biological arguments for racial superiority were thrown into disrepute and overt expressions of racism were discredited, many of the assumptions of racial thinking were maintained intact – in particular the belief that humanity can be divided into discrete groups, that each group should be considered in its own terms, and that differences, not commonalities, shaped human interaction. These assumptions, however, were cast not in biological terms but in the language of cultural pluralism. Pluralism provided a vocabulary with which to articulate social differences without having to refer to the discredited discourse of race. It provided both a sense of continuity with prewar racial discourse and a means of asserting the aversion to racism that exemplified the postwar years.

We have seen how the concept of a plural society developed in the prewar years out of anthropological studies of colonial society. In the postwar world it became refashioned in response to the impact of mass immigration into Western societies. Eleven million workers came to Europe in the 1950s and 1960s, encouraged by an economic boom. In the USA a different kind of mass migration took place – the huge movement of African-Americans to the Northern cities in the 1950s and 1960s. In both cases the newcomers found themselves on the margins of society, subject to racism and discrimination, and unable to gain access to levers of power. The ideology of pluralism developed as an accommodation to the persistence of inequalities despite the rhetoric of integration, assimilation and equality. As immigrant and black communities remained ghettoised, excluded from mainstream society, subject to discrimination and clinging to old habits and lifestyles as a familiar anchor in a hostile world, so such differences became rationalised, not as the negative product of racism or discrimination, but as the positive result of a plural society. In the nineteenth century, the persistence of inequalities had led to the emergence of the discourse of race, in which economic, social and technological differences between groups were attributed to natural distinctions. In the postwar years the persistence of inequalities in the context of mass immigration led to the development of a pluralist outlook, in which differences were welcomed as expressions of cultural diversity.

In the America of the 1960s, for instance, most commentators, both black and white, hoped and expected that African-American migrants to the North would eventually integrate into US society, as fully as had European immigrants. The title of a 1966 article by Irving Kristol in the *New York Times* captured that hope – 'The Negro Today is like the Immigrant Yesterday'.[16] Three decades later it has become obvious how misplaced were such claims. Virtually every social statistic – from housing segregation to rates of intermarriage, from infant mortality rates to language use – shows that African-Americans live very different lives to the rest of America. The experience even of Hispanic-Americans is far closer to that of American whites than it is to that of African-Americans.[17]

As the possibilities of equality seemed more and more constrained, so there was an increasing tendency to celebrate 'difference'. The black American critic bell hooks observes that 'civil rights reform reinforced the idea that black liberation should be defined by the degree to which black people gained equal access to material opportunities and privileges to whites – jobs, housing, schooling etc.' This strategy could never bring about liberation, argues hooks, because such 'ideas of "freedom" were informed by efforts to imitate the behaviour, lifestyles and most importantly the values and consciousness of white colonisers.'[18] The failure of equality has led radical critics like hooks to declare that equality itself is problematic because African-Americans are 'different' from whites.

Politicians and policy-makers have responded to such arguments by reinventing America as a 'plural' or 'multicultural' nation. Pluralism is premised on the idea that America is a nation composed of many different

16. Irving Kristol, 'The Negro today is like the immigrant yesterday', *New York Times Magazine*, 11 September 1966.

17. See, for example, Douglas S. Massey and Nancy A. Denton, *American Apartheid: segregation and the making of the underclass*, Harvard University Press, Cambridge, Massachusetts 1993; Melvin L. Oliver and Thomas M. Shapiro, *Black Wealth/White wealth: a new perspective on racial inequality*, Routledge, London 1995; Andrew Hacker, *Two Nations: black and white, separate, hostile, unequal*, Scribners's, New York City 1992.

18. bell hooks, *Yearning: race, gender and cultural politics*, Turnabout, London 1991, p15.

cultural groups and peoples. But in reality it is the product of the continued exclusion of one group: African-Americans. The promotion of pluralism is a tacit admission that the barriers that separate blacks and whites cannot be breached and that equality has been abandoned as a social policy goal. 'Multiculturalism', Nathan Glazer has written, 'is the price America is paying for the inability or unwillingness to incorporate into its society African–Americans, in the same way and to the same degree it has incorporated so many other groups.'[19] The real price, however, is being paid by African-Americans themselves. For in truth America is not plural or multicultural; it is simply *unequal*. And the promotion of pluralism is an acknowledgement of the inevitability of that inequality. Indeed, in his own way, Glazer himself recognises this. 'We must pass through a period in which we recognise difference, we celebrate difference', he writes, because of 'our failure to integrate blacks.'[20]

19. Nathan Glazer, *We Are All Multiculturalists Now*, Harvard University Press, Cambridge, Massachussets 1997, p147.

20. *Ibid.*, p15

The 'apartness' of black and immigrant communities in Western Europe is probably not so great as that of African-Americans in the USA. Nevertheless, here too pluralism has become a means to avoid debate about the failure of equality. Many young people in Marseilles or East London call themselves Muslim, for instance, less because of religious faith or cultural habits, than because in the face of a hostile, anti-Muslim society, calling oneself Muslim is a way of defending the dignity of one's community. Young Muslims are often not religious; they have mores and outlooks and habits little different from that of their white peers. But racism imposes difference upon them and forces them to adopt difference themselves. Their Islam is not the free celebration of an identity, but an attempt to negotiate a difficult relationship with a hostile society as best they can. In celebrating such cultural differences, we are in danger of celebrating the differences imposed by a racist society, not identities freely chosen by those communities.

I am not, of course, objecting to pluralism in the sense of a society in which there exists the right to free and open political, cultural and religious expression. Rather, what I fear is the one-sided embrace of 'difference' and denigration of universalistic concepts. The irony is that the blind pursuit of pluralism undermines our capacity to defend those very rights of free expression. Such rights can only be defended through a defence of equality. In an equal society, our universal capacity to act as political subjects can take a myriad of forms, and hence can become the basis of true difference. Indeed, only in an equal society can difference have any meaning, because it is only here that difference can be freely chosen. In an unequal society, however, the pursuit of difference all too often means the entrenching of inequalities. Inequalities simply become reframed through the discourse of difference. In such circumstances, there is little possibility of true freedom to express one's political, cultural or religious identities.

A pluralist might reply that the principle of 'difference' implies a truly radical egalitarianism, because it recognises no standard by which one individual or group can be judged as better than another. But the point is that this principle of difference cannot provide any standards which oblige us to respect the 'difference' of others. At best, it invites our indifference to the fate of the Other. At worst, it licenses us to hate and abuse those who are different. Why, after all, should we not abuse and hate them? On what basis can they demand our respect or we demand theirs? It is very difficult to support respect for difference without appealing to some universal principles of equality or social justice. And it is the possibility of establishing just such universal principles that has been undermined by the embrace of a pluralist outlook.

The dangers of a pluralist outlook are much more acute today. Through much of the postwar period, the pernicious impact of pluralism upon the struggle for equality was kept in check. From liberation struggles in the third world to the civil rights movement in the USA, there were vigorous social struggles for equality. The demise of such struggles over the past decade, however, has sapped the morale of anti-racists. Campaigning for equality means challenging accepted practices, being willing to march against the grain, to believe in the possibility of social transformation. Conversely, celebrating differences between peoples allows us to accept society as it is – it says little more than 'We live in a diverse world, enjoy it'.

The social changes that have swept the world over the past decade have intensified this sense of pessimism. The end of the Cold War, the collapse of the left, the fragmentation of the postwar order, the defeat of most liberation movements in the third world and the demise of social movements in the West, have all transformed political consciousness. In particular, they have thrown into question the possibility of social transformation. In this context the quest for equality has increasingly been abandoned in favour of the claim to a diverse society. I suggested previously that the narrative of race was also the narrative of the containment of movements for social emancipation. Much the same may be said about pluralism. The celebration of difference is an intellectual outlook that has been forged out of the seeming impossibility of transforming social relations. It is the product of political defeat, and in particular the product of the defeat of movements for social equality. But the very pursuit of pluralism has itself helped constrain the possibilities of social change, for, in the absence of a universalistic outlook, and in an increasingly fragmented world, the promise of any form of collective action becomes increasingly chimerical. Unless we challenge the blind pursuit of difference, our capacity for meaningful social change will continue to become ever more diminished.

[RACIAL] EQUALITY AND THE POLITICS
OF DIFFERENCE

Nira Yuval-Davis

Debates around issues of equality and difference have been haunting all social movements which have been fighting exclusion and disadvantage in the last twenty years, whether it was women, the disabled or racial and ethnic minorities. On one end of the continuum stand those, often identified with the 'Old Left', the French Republican tradition – and recently, in Britain, Kenan Malik – who see any politics of difference as a relativising and divisive discourse.[1] The problem with this approach, as Balibar and others have pointed out, is that the 'universalist' approach which they support ignores the differential positionings of those to which the universalist rules are supposed to apply and their consequent differential perspectives and needs.[2]

At the other end of the spectrum stand those who endorse and promote a notion of a society based on difference. This notion of difference resulted in the promotion of identity politics. Rosalind Brunt, for instance, has argued that:

> Unless the question of identity is at the heart of any transformatory project, then not only will the political agenda be inadequately 'rethought' but more to the point, our politics aren't going to make much headway beyond the Left's own circles.[3]

'Identity politics' tend, however, to homogenize and naturalize social categories and groupings, as well as to deny shifting boundaries of identities and internal power differences and conflicts of interest.[4] It is important to emphasize, as Paul Gilroy has done, that such an essentialist construction can also be a result of a 'strategic essentialism' of Gayatari Spivak's variety where, while it is acknowledged that such categories involve 'arbitrary closures' (to use a term I've heard used by Stuart Hall), for political mobilization, these categories become reified via practices of social movements and state policies.[5] Rejecting such reified construction does not negate, however, the primary importance that considerations of individual and collective positionings should have in the construction of any political alliances.

In the discourse of race equality, discrimination and disadvantage tend to be collapsed together. The fact that there is a growing black middle class does not make the fate of the black poor any better – maybe just less visible. Moreover, those in the most vulnerable position these days in Britain

1. Kenan Malik, *The Meaning of Race*, Macmillan, London 1996.

2. Etiènne Balibar, 'Paradoxes of Universality', in D.T. Goldberg (ed), *Anatomy of Racism*, University of Minneapolis Press, Minneapolis, Minnesota 1990.

3. Rosalind Brunt, 'The politics of Identity' in Stuart Hall and Martin Jacques (eds), *New Times*, Lawrence & Wishart, London 1989.

4. Floya Anthias and Nira Yuval-Davis, *Racialized Boundaries*, Routledge, London 1992.

5. Gayatri Chakravorty Spivak, *Outside the Teaching Machine*, Routledge, London 1993; Paul Gilroy, *The Black Atlantic*, Verso, London 1993.

often would not be blacks at all – or at least not blacks from the original category around which the British 'race relations industry' has been constructed since the 1970s, but refugees and migrants from other war-ridden and famine-ridden areas of the world. At the same time it has also to be recognized that because of the more and more efficient walls of 'Fortress Europe', many of those who do manage to come are those who are better off and manage to overcome blockages to escape their country of origin. If anybody can prove that they have £50,000 or more at their disposal when they arrive in this country, origin or colour stops playing such an important role and they are allowed to settle here.

Class, however, plays a role in other contexts. When people can afford to pay for private school or private health care, the effects of discrimination are muted. And although black male youth of whatever class origin have a higher chance of being arrested by the police, it is the inner-city underclass which is their prime target.

It is not only class but also gender which is crucial to understanding racist exclusions and practices. Granting asylum on the basis of sex-persecution has been recognized to date only in Canada. Moreover, often the wife and children of a political activist are defined as his dependants with no independent status as asylum-seekers. If he dies they have no legal grounds for claiming refuge, even though the wife might often have been a political activist in her own right and even though, as the widow of a wanted man, she might still be persecuted by the authorities in her own country.

The construction of women as primarily wives and mothers has also been very important in understanding relationships between the police and black communities in Britain. At least two of the major riots in London have erupted when police killed the mothers of their 'wanted men' while searching for the men. The importance of gender in the discourse around riots relates, of course, not only to constructions of womanhood but also to constructions of manhood. One of the most important contradictions that black and minority women have to confront results from the fact that many (if not most) black men have understood Frantz Fanon's call for the black man to reclaim his manhood as a call for aggressive macho-ism rather than as a call for developing a sense of self-worth and assertiveness.

In his talk on the first day of the conference, Stuart Hall commented on the fact that black politics do not take the form of community struggles these days. However, this does not mean that there is a communal vacuum. It is often filled, on the one hand, by religious fundamentalist organizations such as the Nation of Islam, who have been working in places like the Broadwater Farm Estate, and on the other hand, by a whole army of equal opportunity, race and women units and advisors who are there to determine for the state what are the specific needs of the different communities. And although the reality of the lives of the various ethnic minorities in Britain is diverse, and the strategies of survival are individualistic, it is the logic of multiculturalism to assume that all members of a specific community share the same relationship to the same culture. However, as Trin-Min Ha has commented, there are two kinds of social and cultural differences: those which threaten and those which don't. Multi-culturalism is aimed at nourishing and perpetuating the kind of differences which do *not* threaten. Phil Cohen graphically described this in his talk, when he told about Mrs Ntolo's mud hut in the back yard in Becontree, which could only be accepted once the mud was 'normalized' by being covered by concrete.

At the same time multi-culturalist constructions do not have space for internal power conflicts and interest differences within the minority collectivity. They tend to assume collective boundaries which are fixed, static, a-historical and essentialist, with no space for growth and change. When such a perspective becomes translated into social policy, 'authenticity' can become an important political resource with which economic and other resources can be claimed from the state, a line of argument which can lead to unanticipated collusion with fundamentalist leaderships.

During the last few years, however, authenticity has been constructed in apparently very different ways. Phil Cohen mentioned yesterday the Malibu ad. I was struck by the ads for curry sauces, in which the actors, wearing 'authentic' Asian clothes, speak with a Liverpudlian or cockney accents. This might seem, on first sight, to be in opposition to multiculturalism because it celebrates hybridity. However, the trouble with this reading derives from the problematic idea of hybridity itself. The notion of hybridity is that it assumes distinct 'authentic' sources from which the hybrid is composed. For the 'third space' of hybridity to exist, the first and second spaces as fixed authentic structures need to be assumed to have existed socially and historically; in other words, it brings back identity politics and essentialist cultural constructions through the back door.

Rather than a fixed and homogenous body of tradition and custom, culture needs to be described as a rich resource, usually full of internal contradictions, used selectively by different social agents in various projects within specific power relations and political discourses in and outside the collectivity. Gender, class, membership in a collectivity, stage in the life cycle, ability – all affect the access and availability of these resources and the specific positionings from which they are used.

It is important, therefore, to differentiate and avoid the conflation of cultural discourse, identity-narratives and ethnic processes.[6] Identities – individual and collective – are specific forms of cultural narratives which constitute commonalities and differences between self and others, interpreting their social positioning in more or less stable ways.[7] These often relate to myths (which may or may not be historically valid) of common origin, and to myths of common destiny. However, as Stuart Hall points out, cultural identities are often fluid and cross-cutting.[8] This instability of categories can provide us with an important insight into the politics of difference.

6. Nira Yuval-Davis, 'Women, ethnicity and empowerment' in K. Bhavnani and A. Phoenix (eds), *Shifting Identities, Shifting Racisms*, Sage, London 1994; and Nira Yuval-Davis, *Gender and Nation*, Sage, London 1997.

7. Denis-Constans Martin, 'The choices of identity', *Social Identities*, 1:1, 1995.

8. Stuart Hall, 'New Ethnicities' in J. Donald and Ali Rattansi (eds), *Race, Culture and Difference*, Sage, London 1992.

Identity-narratives often constitute major tools of ethnic projects. Ethnicity relates to the politics of collective boundaries, a means to divide the world into 'us' and 'them'. Ethnic projects are continuously engaged in processes of struggle and negotiation aimed, from specific positionings within the collectivities, at promoting the collectivity or perpetuating its advantages, via access to the institutions of state and civil society.[9]

Ethnicity, according to this definition is, therefore, primarily a political process which constructs the collectivity and 'its interest', not only as a result of the general positioning of the collectivity in relation to others in the society, but also as a result of the specific relations of those engaged in 'ethnic politics' with others within that collectivity. Gender, class, political, religious and other differences play central roles in the construction of specific ethnic politics and different ethnic projects. Some of these projects can involve different constructions of the actual boundaries of the collectivity as, for example, has been the case in the debate about the boundaries of the 'black' community in Britain.[10] Ethnicity is not specific to oppressed and minority groupings. On the contrary, one of the measures of the success of hegemonic ethnicities is the extent to which they succeed in 'naturalizing' their social and cultural constructions.

Ethnic projects mobilize all available relevant resources for their promotion. Some of these resources are political, others are economic and yet others are cultural – relating to customs, language, religion and other cultural artifacts and memories. Class, gender, political and personal differences mean that people positioned differently within the collectivity could, while pursuing specific ethnic projects, sometimes use the same cultural resources for promoting opposite political goals (for example using various Koran surras to justify pro- and anti- legal abortion politics, as was the case in Egypt; or using rock music to mobilize people for or against the extreme Right in Britain). In other times, different cultural resources are used to legitimize competing ethnic projects of the collectivity – for example when Bundists used Yiddish as 'the' Jewish language, in an ethnic-national project whose identity-boundaries were to include East European Jewry, and when Zionists re-invented modern Hebrew in order to include in their project Jews from all over the world. Similarly in Britain, the same people can be constructed by different ethnic-racist political projects to be 'Paki', 'black Asians', or 'Muslim fundamentalists'.

Thus it is clear why ethnicity cannot be reduced to culture, and why 'culture' cannot be seen as a fixed, essentialist category. As Aleksandra Alund comments, 'the tendency to conflate ethnicity and culture leads to inability to attend to the political dynamics of ethnic difference'.[11] Moreover, defining and differentiating between culture, identity and ethnicity in this way pre-empts debates on the notion of 'authenticity'. Authenticity assumes fixed, essential and unitary constructs of cultures, identities and groupings. 'Authentic voices' are perceived as their 'true' representatives. As we shall see when discussing identity politics and

9. Nira Yuval-Davis, *Gender and Nation*, op. cit..

10. Tariq Modood, '"Black", racial equality and Asian identity' *New Community* 14:3, 1988; Tariq Modood, 'Political blackness and British Asians', *Sociology* vol 28, 1994; Avtar Brah, 'Difference, diversity, differentiation', *International Review of Sociology*, New Series 2, 1991.

11. Aleksandra Alund, 'Alterity in Modernity', *Acta Sociologica*, 38, 1995.

12. Amrita Chachhi,
'Forced Identities:
the state, communal-
ism, fundamentalism
and women in
India', in D.
Kandiyoti (ed),
*Women, Islam & the
State*, Macmillan,
London 1991; and
Kobena Mercer,
'Welcome to the
jungle: identity and
diversity in post-
modern politics' in
J. Rutherford (ed),
*Identity,
Community,
Culture, Difference*,
Lawrence &
Wishart, London
1990.

13. Patricia Hill-
Collins, *Black
Feminist Thought*,
HarperCollins,
London 1990.

14. Yuval-Davis,
Gender and Nation,
op. cit..

15. Elsa Barkley
Brown, 'African-
American women
quilting: a frame-
work for conceptu-
alizing and teaching
African-American
women's history',
Signs, 14:4, 1989.

16. Alison Assitter,
Enlightened Women,
Routledge, London
1996.

multiculturalism, 'authenticity' can become a political and economic resource in specific ethnic projects, but can also give rise to what Kobena Mercer has called 'the burden of representation' and Amrita Chhachhi, in a different context, has called 'forced identities'.[12]

Instead of identity politics or politics of difference, I would like to suggest the model of transversal politics.

TRANSVERSAL POLITICS

Transversal politics is based on dialogue which takes into account the different positionings of people but does not grant any of them a priori privileged access to the 'truth'. In transversal politics, perceived unity and homogeneity are replaced by dialogues which give recognition to the specific positionings of those who participate in them as well as to the 'unfinished knowledge' (to use Patricia Hill-Collins' term) that each such situated positioning can offer.[13]

Central to transversal politics are the processes which the Italian femi-nists from Bologna's Women's Resource Centre have called 'rooting' and 'shifting'.[14] The idea is that each participant in the dialogue brings with her the rooting in her own grouping and identity, but at the same time tries to shift in order to put herself in a situation of exchange with women who have different groupings and identities.

Two things are vital in developing the transversal perspective. Firstly, that the process of shifting should not involve self de-centring, that is losing one's own rooting and set of values. As Elsa Barkley Brown pointed out – 'one has no need to "decenter" anyone in order to center someone else; one has only to constantly pivot the centre'.[15] It is vital in any form of coalition and solidarity politics to keep one's own perspective on things while empathising with and respecting others. In multiculturalist types of solidarity politics there can be a risk of uncritical solidarity. This was prevalent, for instance, in the politics of some sections of the left around the Iranian revolution or the Rushdie Affair. Some saw it as 'imperialist' and 'racist' to intervene in 'internal community matters'. Women are often the victims of such a perspective which allows the so-called representatives and leaders of 'the community' to determine policies concerning women.

Secondly, the process of shifting should not homogenize the 'other'. As there are diverse positions and points of view among people who are simi-larly rooted, so there are among the members of the other group. The transversal coming together should not be with the members of the other group 'en bloc', but with those who, in their different rooting, share compatible values and goals to one's own, expressed in what Alison Assiter has called 'epistemological communities'.[16] Transversal politics does not assume that the dialogue is without boundaries, or that each conflict of interest is reconcilable. However, the boundaries of such a dialogue are determined by the message, rather than by the messenger. The struggle against oppression and discrimination might (and mostly does) have a specific categorical focus but is never confined just to that category.

A word of caution, however, is required here. A transversal politics is not always possible, as conflicting interests of people who are situated in specific positionings are not always reconcilable. However, when solidarity is possible, it is important that it is based on transversal principles.

RETROSPECT

DISCUSSION WITH BARNOR HESSE,
JAYNE IFEKWUNIGWE AND GUCHARAN VIRDEE

Barnor: What I found interesting about the conference was that it was not something you could evaluate: everyone who went there went to a certain angle, no-one had the overall picture, so what people were doing was making their own involvement in the conference into the conference itself. It created so many happenings, and I think at the end the plenary, where things seemed to fall apart, that was the point at which it was beginning to open up. It was very interesting.

Gucharan: I was very excited about the conference and the planning of it. We wanted a conference with a difference, and I remember being really stressed. We were keen not only to involve academics but also artists, community groups, people who were active on the day-to-day events of cultural politics as well as racism. Our intentions were very exciting, and we were aware that we wanted a multi-media interaction. We had all these bright ideas about using the network, e-mail, video boxes. We were hoping the academics weren't going to take over. It was creating a space for everybody.

Jayne: What was interesting was the parallel way in which issues of content and structure were conceived. We were clear in terms of particular substantive issues that we wanted to debate around cultural politics and identity, and what that means in a non-essential way, but also in terms of the form. It was exciting that people were open to different ways of delivering particular ideas and issues, in the form of film, music, performance, poetry. The strands themselves, in terms of the topics covered, interacted and complemented each other in a powerful way.

Barnor: Let me raise a more sceptical note about some of the connections between politics and race. I've always had a problem about the way the debate about essentialism has gone. I think it has reached the point where it is a non-debate. There isn't a point there, everybody debates essentialism and often does it from a set of positions which are so heavily essentialised and fixed and clearly defined through a boundary, or some kind of frontier, as to make that whole debate fatuous.

I think what was happening at the conference was that we've reached a point within the academic discourse where there is a great deal of investment in talking about the category of race, but not racism, and among the so-called grass-roots or activists, most of their fixations are on questions of racism. That's where I saw the mismatch. One of the issues that came up in my own session was: 'How do you begin to talk about racism, because it's no longer about questions of power and politics, it's about people's identities, cultural identities?' So the academic discourse, I would argue, has culturalised the issues to such an extent that politics begins to evaporate. The people who are the so-called grass-roots activists are grappling with the politics and finding that the language of academia does not allow a door to be entered through which that politics could be undertaken. If you look at the shifts that have taken place in the 1990s, it's virtually impossible to find a language that speaks about racism as if it has an impact. In fact, I'd go so far as to argue that many of the analyses now treat the social conditions in Britain, or even in the West, as if we're living in a post-racist condition. And we're not. Many of the things which have been raised by racial attacks are still on the agenda, but academic discourse simply ignores them.

Jayne: What has been smuggled in to cover up the fact that we're still living within a racist state is that wonderful term called 'hybridity', in particular 'cultural hybridity'. This was particularly apparent for me in the discussion of mixed race identities. On the one hand you have people claiming 'I am-ism', the sense that I'm not black, I'm not white, I'm me. And there is this other sense that race has incredible power as racism. So how do we reconcile the fact that race is this idea that doesn't really speak to our biological, genetic realities, but on the other hand, it identifies us (as mixed race people) as black, and as a result we experience racism.

Barnor: Well, let's go back to the metaphor of frontlines and backyards. There are so many ways you can read the metaphor of frontlines, and backyards are ways of disrupting the potential fixity of frontlines. We understand modern politics in terms of constructing frontiers, creating a friend and a foe distinction, in order to organise our sense of what the good life might be, or what the question is *vis-a-vis* the deportment of people's individual rights. So in any contested situation we're going to find people taking up positions, and they take up positions in order to advocate certain arguments and make certain analyses, which they have to fight for. The problem is that's the way modern politics has been constructed. *Creating* the politics of frontline positions. How do you think away from that?

Jayne: Yet what was brought to the forefront in my experience of the conference was the sense of multiple localities, the sense that it wasn't possible for individuals in a territorial sense, by virtue of multiple nationalities and transnationalities, necessarily to locate themselves in one particular position. It was actually that sense of fault lines which was most significant – this way in which notions of boundaries, and exclusion and inclusion, would have to be ruptured in order to include the lived experiences of individuals who embody seemingly disparate realities.

Gucharan: What was interesting in one of the discussions I went to, the one looking at the Kurdish issue, was the way the Kurdish speakers had brought the borders of their homelands back into Britain. They were looking at the issue of how they felt placed here, talking about it on a local level. Yet even so, masculine issues remained at the forefront. Nobody was prepared to talk about gender, about the effects of war, about rape, about what happens to women within those situations. They were very keen to keep to the frontlines as being male and affecting men, and as soon as it came to gender they said: 'It's culture, or religion, we don't want to talk about it'. I found that disturbing. I thought we'd moved along, and yet it seems that we move forward and then backwards in terms of these frontlines/backyards. Some issues are quite open in the ways they're talked about; in other ways they get repressed, excluded, and become exclusive.

Jayne: I wonder if we would have had a different response if we had not created that dialectic, if we had just called it Frontlines.
    Yet in the Multiple Occupancies discussions the focus was looking at the experiences of individuals who embody more than one cultural reality. And what was exciting about that perspective was that it was able to draw in a lot of individuals who in some shape or form saw themselves as multiracial or *metis* or mixed-race or whatever. Many through the course of the day spoke of this space that we had created as the first time they had experienced communities, the first time they had been in a public space where they felt legitimated.

Gucharan: That also means something positive about young people, because it was noticeable that the participants were quite young, college and university leavers. I'm not saying they were exclusively that, but there was a sense that they didn't have a forum to debate a lot of the issues, not only about cultural identity and identity politics, but even about racism, or some of the other issues that we had strands on, such as community politics, refugees, etc.

Jayne: The sadness is that I left thinking: what's going to happen next? We need to network, and sadly, because of other commitments it hasn't happened. So there is a sense of an anti-climax almost, at least for me.

Barnor: There were a lot of subterranean dialogues, in fact probably the whole conference was a series of subterranean activities. What it revealed to me – and it was unique, because I've not attended any event like that – was that we've reached an impasse. The conference, in terms of problematising frontlines and backyards, was signifying the fact that there isn't an overall language for it. So how do we talk about these issues in the absence of an overall language? The conference provided a number of people with the opportunity to find a language of sorts, which is why people stayed with their own workshops. When we tried to have the plenary at the end it was like the Tower of Babel. The reason I say there was an impasse was because it was clear that although there isn't an overall language, there is a dominant framework for talking about these issues, but one which has sidelined many of the approaches to them.

Gucharan: It's true. The plenary was also a bit of an impasse. Perhaps that is why it has proved difficult subsequently to create appropriate networks deriving from the conference.

Jayne: That is also the question of what it means to privilege one form of knowledge over another – knowledge in the sense of how ideas are communicated, whether through visual images, music, poetry, personal testimony, or through an academic discourse. Can we digest these discourses on an equal plane? What was saddening about the final session was that it returned unproblematically to conventional academic discourses.

Barnor: But a serious problem was also the way in which this academicism occludes really critical issues. One of the key things I tried to pick up and develop was the curious idea – I know it is a minority position that I seem to occupy with very few people – that somehow the end of the twentieth century has constructed a position in which the history that produces racism has been sanitised, such that we can no longer speak of a history producing racism. In order to begin to talk about racism, we cannot anchor that in a historical discussion at all. A curious thing happens to the history of Britain after the slave trade: slavery becomes immaterial to Britain. In a post-colonial situation, after the colonial empire had collapsed, the empire is immaterial to Britain's history. So then we get into a narrower and narrower space in which we can talk about race and racism, and that becomes post-war migration. And then suddenly we're in a position in the 1990s where even that is no longer relevant. So we go to a position of what I call political relativism, which is that people are simply in different racialised positions, and the politics arises simply from being in a different position.

   Anyway, I've always hated plenaries where people report back, it's so functional, it's bureaucratic.

Jayne: Well there is another model, where we claim the space that was occupied for the day. There was a moment of community, which was dissolved more quickly than it need have been.

Barnor: Maybe I need to be clearer about what I meant by an impasse. There is a divergence of political languages which enables us not to talk about certain issues at the same time. For example, not to be able to talk about equality *and* difference at the same time, or questions of cultural representation and material, social and economic issues. The second thing that needs to be done is to actually look at what sort of forces work against that naming process, or having that sort of discussion. I certainly think it is the case now, as I said earlier, that part of the current social formation of racism is a series of mechanisms which prevent people from recognising it, from naming it, from actually describing its impact in Britain. It is a logic of disavowal.

Jayne: There's also the sense that issues are in and of themselves more complex than simply naming a form of discrimination, such as racism. Which isn't to say that I'm invalidating racism as a significant institution in British society. But I also feel that there are complex issues that are contained within this institution that are never then necessarily addressed. We can look at racism as a form of inter-group conflict. But we are coming closer to acknowledging the fact that there are intra-group tensions around colourism, sexism, class discrimination, nationalism, tribalism, which are then contained and suppressed by this dominant discourse of racism.

Barnor: I'm not saying that we need to talk about the primacy of racism; what I'm saying is that, given the conference and that the reason we're here is to talk about issues of race and racism, let's look at the ways we have in fact been talking about them.

Jayne: But was that the objective of the conference?

Barnor: Irrespective of the naming of the conference, what was signified to people was: 'Here is a conference about race and racism'. Race and racism operated as the co-ordinates, and the point I want to make is that, given that they were dominant co-ordinates, they never really got spoken about.

Jayne: I disagree with you that they were dominant co-ordinates.

Barnor: It seems to me that if you had said to the people there: 'This conference is not about race and racism', it would have fallen apart.

Jayne: And nationalism, and ethnicity, and gender – you're homogenising a very complex issue.

Barnor: Because I think it's race and racism that are constitutive of the links between all those different issues, at least in terms of the confererence. If nobody passed through the eye of the needle marked 'race', they wouldn't have had any way of talking to each other.

Gucharan: Wasn't that one of the conference aims, to talk about why the politics have gone out of cultural politics and identity issues? We *have* had the language to talk about race and racism, but it's shifting all the time. I'm wondering what that shift is about, because I think it does depoliticise the whole issue of race and racism.

Barnor: The irony is, as we expand the discourse to be able to think questions of difference, what I have noticed is that the capacity to talk about a name in the issue of race and racism has been dissipated. And that's partly why the politics has gone out of it. When you were saying about racism being inter-group conflict, that's part of what I'm talking about, a relativising of –

Jayne: No, you only took part of my statement. I was saying there are other forms of conflict that need to be addressed, as well as a form of conflict that is predicated on biology and domination.

Barnor: OK. I suppose what I'm saying is: if we've made a commitment to look at certain issues, and race is part of that, and racism is central, how does racism cease to be central? In the conference racism wasn't central.

Jayne: You've just said it was!

Barnor: As a set of co-ordinates. But as a substantive issue –

Jayne: You're only talking about the discussions you organized. I would say the historical sessions addressed race, the refugee strand addressed race, my strand did – how can you say it wasn't a central issue? And racism.

Barnor: One of the arguments I'm making is that the focus is on race rather than on racism. You can have something which is central in its absence, and that's what I meant by a co-ordinate. We can talk about race *as if* there were not questions of power and domination and inequalities which are structured by racism. And increasingly, I think, that's what's happening. People are saying 'Race – and racism', and it's the 'and racism' that is dissipated.

Jayne: I don't feel we should sell ourselves short by presuming that these issues weren't addressed, because I feel they were: maybe not named and claimed and framed in the way that you would like them to be, but in different ways they were addressed.

Gucharan: Well, in the future I would hope that we could address more directly the question of youth, on the one hand, and on the other the whole question of a new black middle class in Britain, and its various political forms. I'd like to explore those kinds of issues, what do they really mean in terms of cultural politics and current politics, and with New Labour.

Jayne: I think one way out of the impasse is to focus on hybridity and its formations, biological and cultural. That would be a way, perhaps a historiographic way, to problematise race and racism in interesting ways. It would be a way to access cultural politics of difference, but also the history of race as an idea and how it became racism and racialisation.

Barnor: I would be interested in looking at two sets of questions: one, how do we connect the politics of identity and difference to the politics of social institutions and social formations? The second question would be: how do we address questions which aim to sever that kind of link? Let me give you an example: it's still amazing that if you pick up a book about racism in Britain, the average textbook, you find invariably there's nothing about racial violence and racial attacks; if you get to a position where there is something about racial violence, somehow that has no connection with the construction of British national identity. So we're then forced into a situation in which we either look at some kind of minute social institution as a kind of beyond-the-pale Britishness, various fascist sects for example, or particular urban locations, or we look at individual formations of group identity. For me it's that kind of breach that has to be healed. I think the conference was very good at raising the issues in which people could affiliate to construction of their own identity; but in terms of creating a politics in relation to these social institutions, I think that's where analytical work is lacking.

POST-COLONIAL AMBIGUITY

Benita Parry

Simon Gikandi, *Maps of Englishness: Writing Identity in the Culture of Colonialism*, Columbia University Press, New York 1997, 268pp; $49.50 cloth, $17.50 paperback.

The recent proliferation of studies on the overt and cryptic dissemination of empire in English cultural life, has expanded the frame within which a range of metropolitan representational forms and social practices can now be discussed. It has also, in the interest of establishing the historical conjunction and mutual imbrication between ruler and ruled, extended the definition of 'the colonial subject' to include all who were constructed by colonialist ideology. In the words of Simon Gikandi, the experience of colonialism constituted 'the conditions of possibility for metropolitan and colonial subjects and cultures alike' (p191). One consequence of this move has been to foster the notion that colonialism *determined* the invention of Englishness.

Perhaps this condensation of a causal relationship is a response to the long neglect of colonialism in dissident rewritings of the making of English culture and society. However, to recognize that overseas empire was constitutive of the domestic space in ways material, symbolic and psychic does not substantiate the incautious assertion that the imperial project was the sole agency of metropolitan subject reformation in an age of accelerated modernization which also saw an intensification of class struggles, the emergence of a proto-feminism, and upheavals in cognitive modes precipitated by the revolution in scientific knowledge and technology. Hence, any proposition concerning a national subjectivity must recognize the role of other factors in producing what were articulations of disjunctive experiential registers: class location and political alignment, attachments to regional, religious and ethical communities, gender position and sexual affiliation, as well as self-definitions inflected by perceptions of resident aliens such as Jews and other minorities. A related reduction of the tangled web of causations is implicit in the assertion that the structures and codes of the colonial episteme also *determined* the identities of the colonized.

These axioms underpin the formal thesis of Gikandi's book. His brief is to trace the construction and securing of Englishness in the spaces of imperial alterity within a shared colonial culture; the verso to this narrative is the story of the colonized's self-representation which, he asserts, could only be written within the totality established by empire: 'Empire *robbed* colonial subjects of their identities ... but it also *conferred* new forms of identity on native peoples' (p191). (My emphasis: to indicate the allocation of all power to the dominant ideology, a matter to which I will return). As I understand Gikandi's study, its achievement lies in exceeding the constraints of such *données* on the authority of colonialism's culture over 'consciousness, ideology and even language' in both metropole and colony.

The significant readings of Carlyle, Trollope and Froude, Mary Kingsley, Conrad and Graham Greene offered by Gikandi demonstrate both complicity and transgression *vis-à-vis* the authorized version, and his nuanced discussions are alert to the agency of the texts in inventing, underwriting, defamiliarizing and destabilizing colonialism's assertion of ascendancy. What emerges is that far more than English identity was secured in those writings which were instrumental interventions in legitimizing colonialism, and subverted in those which ventured critiques. Other critics may select different texts, but their discoveries will re-iterate his findings on both the entry of colonial spaces into multiple and contradictory discourses of Englishness, the tropological structure to the rhetorics of imperial authority, and the tortuous languages of nonconformity.

In Gikandi's discussion of Conrad's African writings, and in particular *Heart of Darkness*, the fictions are shown to perform the shift from the relative stability of realism in the English novel to the anxiety of modernist style. Here Gikandi, who locates changing inscriptions of empire in novelistic practice, examines how the novella, by relinquishing cognitive authority, narrates the failure of once-hegemonic theories of representation. This reading reprises the movement of Gikandi's book from the consolidation of empire as referent during the nineteenth century, to its 'state of terminal decline' (p164) in the modernist period. However, *pace* Gikandi, metropolitan anxieties about empire cannot be wholly attributed to the destabilizing of English identity precipitated by the collapse of colonialism's discursive structures. For social theorists, commentators and novelists such as J. A. Hobson, C. F. G. Masterman, H. G. Wells and Conrad, it was the aggressive pursuit of imperialist interests and the enthusiasm for empire this engendered in the populace, which were perceived as deleterious to the moral condition of the homeland.

By his declared stance, Gikandi situates himself within the mainstream of postcolonial theory, and by inference he affiliates his work to the dominant tendency in contemporary cultural studies. To cite one commentator, it is by now abundantly evident that despite its 'materialist inspiration', cultural studies have moved 'to an essentially textualist account of culture',[1] displaying an exclusive interest in culturally-based explanations of social processes, and giving little or no heed to material practices and historical conditions. A move away from social explanations of both the symbolic order and historical events has prompted Nancy Fraser to call for a restoration of political economy to its proper place in critical theory. Her argument is that the distinction is an analytical one, since in practice material processes are shot through with significations, and cultural practices

1. See Colin Sparks, 'Stuart Hall, Cultural Studies and Marxism', in David Morley and Kuan-Hsing Chen (eds), *Stuart Hall: Critical Dialogues in Cultural Studies*, Routledge, London 1996, pp71-101; pp97, 98.

are never without political and economic dimensions.[2] Fraser then urges that the material and the symbolic be conceived of as interactive spheres, and she does so without denying the importance of attending to the exercise of signifyng power.

Nowhere are the consequences of the discursive turn more apparent than in those postcolonial rewritings of colonialism and its aftermath from which modern empire as a coercive project of an expansionist western capitalism is absent. Where colonialism was the object of socio-economic and political examination, discussion of its elaborate strategies of legitimation and disseminated effects on the making of both metropolitan and colonial cultures, was secondary to questions of empire's economic trajectory, military conquests, exploitation of colonial labour and resources and institutional rule. With the new dispensation, the notion of colonialism as a system of power and control has become detached from its genesis in European expansionism and its consequences in facilitating the uneven insertion of once-colonized worlds into a global capitalist economy. Such erasures permit Simon Gikandi to cite at face value Nicholas Dirks' proposition that 'culture was what colonialism was all about' (p xi). (While faulting explanations which displace a cultural project of control 'into the inexorable logic of modernization and world capitalism', Dirks modulates his statements with references to the colonizer's military superiority, political power and economic wealth).[3]

Because Gikandi construes colonialism as a cultural project, his analysis is drained of the categories of political economy and structural political conflict, and this permits him to contend that 'the resonance of empire lay in its ability to evoke a horizontal identity for both the colonizer and the colonized even when they were imprisoned in strict racial and economic hierarchies' (p191). This same culturalist paradigm also prompts him to connect a collapse in the stability of 'the image of empire', with what he claims were the always 'unstable structures of empire' even when Britannia ruled the waves, thereby suggesting a homologous relationship between textuality and the historical world. But because colonial rule was not fragile until threatened by colonial struggles and changes within metropolitan state formations, this points rather to a disjunction between the discursive uncertainties of *fin-de-siècle* fiction, which can be read as a troubled literary response to a condition, and the energy with which Britain was pursuing territorial acquisition in Africa and implementing intensified bureaucratic rule in India, which were real events. It may also be as well to remember that when writers like Graham Greene registered a sense of imperial decline and deployed the figure of Africa to express their disenchantment with western civilization, Britain continued to fight colonial wars in defence of its empire.

The stated 'political motive' of Gikandi's study is to transcend 'the metaphorical and mythological binarism promoted by empire' (p17), and by rejecting the colonial borderland as victimized margin without a voice

2. 'Recognition and Redistribution', *New Left Review* 212, July/August 1995, pp 68-93.

3. 'Introduction' to Nicholas Dirks (ed), *Colonialism and Culture*, University of Michigan Press, Ann Arbor 1992, p3.

in shaping events, to recover the agency of the peripheries. To this end he seeks instances of a traffic in cognitive modes from border to centre, citing the acquisition of African languages by missionaries, the reinvigoration of English cultural traditions through the return to British cricket of altered practices devised in the West Indies, and the texts of colonial subjects like Mary Seacole who 'rewrite themselves otherwise', even as they accept their imperial identity. But while foregrounding attenuated or compromised examples of colonial agency, Gikandi appears uninterested in those insurgent voices which *did* indeed 'shape events' – such as *marronage* in the Americas and peasant resistance in India, both of which were spoken in a vernacular idiom during times when Gikandi insists that the colonial subject could only utter what the dominant allowed it to utter (p142).

Furthermore, an anti-colonialism delivered in a modern vocabulary is seriously misconstrued by Gikandi as an atavistic discourse which insisted 'on the integrity and fixity of the national space and its boundaries and the sacredness of its genealogy' (p213), where 'the notion of *tradition*' was privileged (p227), and in which 'the trope of retour ... was lyricised as a gesture of self-affirmation' (p215). But far from failing to break away from the 'grammar of colonial culture', as Gikandi charges, the texts of decolonization to which Marxism was central (see the writings of Césaire, Fanon and Cabral), had deconstructed colonialism's ideology and teleology long before western theory got round to it. Theorists of anti-colonial movements certainly did recognize the significance of recuperating multiply-inflected indigenous cultures from colonialist calumny. But they did not advocate a return to a pre-colonial past, since they were fighting for a future condition in which the material and technical advances, inadvertently effected by colonialism, would be redeployed under egalitarian, postcolonial conditions.

In turning to the subsequent effects of the imperial referent on the writing of identity after colonialism's passing, Gikandi appears to set up the 'alternative narratives' of the decolonizing moment which attempted 'a conscious rejection of an imposed European identity' (p194), against diasporic postcolonial writing where 'the impossibility of detaching oneself from such compromised axioms as empire, cultural nationalism and the postcolony' (p210) is performed in a move to transcend such categories. When Gikandi observes that a writer such as Salman Rushdie appeals to 'the authority of migration and displacement' (p195), and cites Spivak's remark on the migrant imagination not being paradigmatic of 'the historical case of postcoloniality', the reader may be led to anticipate dissent from the privileging of the postcolonial diaspora (p207). Yet his discussion does not extend to the literary production of the 'postcolonies', about which he has written elsewhere, and where very different stories are told of post-independence conditions within the reconstructed nation-state. Instead Gikandi embraces postcolonial theory and writing for its attempt 'to critique and detour the project of the nation, both at home and abroad' (p236 n21) – although he himself makes a 'retour' to notions he has discredited in conceding that 'when all the deconstruction is done, and when all the tropes and figures have been split and hybridized, England and India, like the political realities they have come to represent, insist on their historicity, their social meanings, and configuration of memories and desires' (pp225-6).

Gikandi begins and ends his book with references to 'what at first appeared to be a huge chasm' separating poststructuralist critics of colonialism from Marxists, who are named as empiricists. His conclusion, that the gap now seems to him 'strategic rather than epistemological' (p226), will surprise adherents of both schools; and because he uses the postcolonial interchangeably to signify a condition that does not yet exist (p199), a state of transition and cultural instability (p15), and as descriptive of actual post-independence regimes, his generous move to effect a reconciliation between incommensurable theoretical positions may be a sign of the author's affection for indeterminacy in signification and his casualness towards the categories of materialist analysis.

MAPPING THE SOCIOLOGY OF RACE

Caroline Knowles

John Solomos and Les Back, *Racism and Society*, Macmillan, Basingstoke 1996, 272pp; £12.50 paperback, £40.00 cloth.

The rationale for documenting the changing morphology of racial ideas and practices and evaluating the frameworks used for analysing racialised social relations in social and cultural theory is underscored by the enduring centrality of race at the end of the twentieth century. If Slavoj Zizek's chilling comment (p211) that the former Yugoslavia is not an anachronism but our first taste of the twenty-first century is anything to go by; and if race and nationalism, as David Theo Goldberg claims (p211), provide a basis of certainty and identity on the shifting landscape of our times, then we can expect the body counts from genocides and ethnic cleansing to go on rising.

Solomos and Back take their readers on a tour of thirty years of theoretical analysis and political action challenging racism – a tour which raises some interesting questions about the relationship between racialised and ethnicised atrocities and the frameworks through which they are grasped. It takes a certain political optimism not to draw the obvious conclusion that the better we *understand* the worse things get, and to set out a research agenda which fills some of the gaps of the last thirty years while not retreating from the theoretical insights which have accumulated and which require that race be understood in ways which pay attention to processes of constant social transformation, to social and political context, to ambiguity and multiplicity, and to local/global dynamics. This book is very much a critical summary of the field, and a bid to move forward in certain directions.

Threaded through the text is the demand for a better understanding of a politics of anti-racism, an agenda which is consistent with the authors' earlier work and which draws on some of the insights of Stephen Feuchtwang.[1] The problem with anti-racist politics, national liberation and black community struggles is that they use what Stuart Hall calls a 'grammar of race' which sustains notions of absolute human difference organized by culture, race and ethnicity: the categories also used by racist discourses to organize forms of social exclusion and privilege. Anti-racism, as the authors point out, must do more than just reverse the imagery of racism. Attempts to move away from the grammar of race prompt a crisis of anti-racist politics. The retreat from Hall's *essential black subject* to the multi-inflected identities of *new ethnicities* as a cultural and intellectual project deals with the fragmentation of black political mobilization by

1. Stephan Feuchtwang, 'Racism: Territoriality and Ethnocentricity' in A. X. Cambridge and Stephan Feuchtwang (eds), *Anti-Racist Strategies*, Averbury, Aldershot 1990.

maintaining racial identity as the 'fiction' which is necessary to make both politics and identity *work*. Solomos and Back (p113) flag the need for a politics which goes beyond opposition mobilized around even fictive racial identities, and which conceives of forms of social being which allow us to live with racialized and ethnicized differences – a truly multi-racial society. Feuchtwang's analysis, which calls for a politics which reasserts forms of humanity and social subjectivity as *citizenship* at the same time as pursuing a practical approach to policy interventions, comes the closest to conceptualizing a positive alternative vision of genuine multi-racialism.

The unresolved problem of the lack of viable alternatives to the social categories mobilized in racist discourse and practice surfaces again as the authors (p152) deal with some of the global/local dynamics of race, noting the intensity of local forms of nationalism which accompany the global transmission of signs, symbols and structures of expression around racialised differences. There is a distinct lack of convincing accounts in social and cultural theory of the racial dynamics of globalisation. From images of Empire and Englishness on biscuit tins and 'glory matches' to the corporate multi-culturalism of Benetton posters, they note the emergence of a transnational advertising aesthetic in which there is an 'unprecedented level of enchantment with difference' (pp159-186). As Kevin Robins says: 'The local and "exotic" are torn out of place and time to be repackaged for the world bazaar' (quoted p185). But the messages of a common and transnational humanity embedded in these images are also premised on notions of absolute racial and cultural difference invoked in racism's categories of personhood, and which reaffirm black people as a 'race apart' (p192). Kobena Mercer rescues popular culture's ambivalence as a site where racist images are both perpetrated and challenged in much the same way as Hall rescues political blackness from the fragmentation of multi-inflected identities, by suggesting that the images of corporate multi-culturalism disturb the racist assumptions of popular culture with aesthetic irony. The tension between racist and anti-racist concepts of social subjectivity and personhood still needs to be resolved both theoretically and politically.

The importance of understanding the racialisation of whiteness, deflecting the analytical gaze away from blackness, is also marked by the authors for further investigation. In societies such as Britain and the United States where racialisation is intense – because race is a factor in how people are seen and treated and consequently in the ways in which they see themselves – there is a proliferation of *racialised* and *ethnicised* identities and forms of subjectivity. The situational development of English ethnicity, and its links with global colonial expansion which fashioned subjectivities in national terms, provides and provokes an interesting empirical discussion of some of the historical aspects of globalisation. The political contexts in which whiteness becomes an object of scrutiny – and which are marked by the authors for analysis – however, are not just about redirect-

2. Robert Blauner quoted in Charles Gallagher, 'White Reconstruction in the University', *Socialist Review*, Vol 24, No 1-2 1995, p181.

3. *Ibid.*, p177.

ing the critical gaze from blackness and challenging the positioning of whiteness as a norm. In the United States, and to some extent in Britain, there is a political momentum to reframe whiteness in more positive terms. This momentum is part of a 'yearning for a useable past':[2] a yearning which has 'resurrected the "white man's burden" at the turn of the twentieth century, only now it is claiming the status of victim.'[3] Clearly, whiteness, also an essentialist category of racist discourse, is invoked by some diverse political projects including the demand to dismantle equality and affirmative action programmes. We need to tread carefully around the politics of whiteness.

That race and racism permeate every social and political exchange has guaranteed their place in the social and cultural theory through which Solomos and Back guide us so eloquently, providing a skilful and thoughtful summary of some of the key intellectual shifts in thirty years of race theory. As well as providing a route-map through some key literature and ideas they sketch out research agendas which stress the need for *empirical research* and a *grounding in politics*. This is a timely reminder. The ubiquity of race, however, is something in which social theory, *as well* as the social trends it seeks to explain, is implicated. The ambiguity of social theory *talking-up* what it criticises and marks for political opposition is also something worthy of discussion. One of the key shifts in British and American race writing is the extent to which racism no longer needs to be demonstrated because it has become an accepted, if not acceptable, part of social landscapes. This embeddedness makes analysing and challenging it yet more difficult. This excellent book also misses an opportunity to extend the existing literature by reflecting further on the social implications of a politics of difference based on citizenship and multi-culturalism which does not rely on essentialist racialised or ethnicised categories.

4. See his 'Racial Formation and Hegemony: Global and Local Developments' in Ali Rattansi and Sallie Westwood (eds), *Racism, Modernity and Identity on the Western Front*, Polity, London 1994.

A broader account of the racial dynamics of globalization – which goes beyond popular culture – is also desperately needed. This is something to which Howard Winant hints at but does not deliver.[4] The focus on popular culture throughout this book, while correctly highlighting the need to understand the racialisation of the banality of everyday life, implicitly directs any potential research agenda away from concern with the racialised forms of social regulation and exclusion which marked sociology in the 1980s. Concern with racial inequalities embedded in forms of social distribution may seem analytically dated, but they are still a serious social and political problem. Finally, there is the troubling relationship between genocidal acts and the development of race theory which suggests that in addition to understanding racism in popular culture we need better accounts of human behaviour.

NOISY ASIANS

Steve Sweeney-Turner

Sanjay Sharma, John Hutnyk and Ashwani Sharma (eds), *Dis-Orienting Rhythms: The Politics of the New Asian Dance Music*, Zed Books, London 1996, 248pp; £12.95 paperback, £45.00 cloth.

> Cultural Studies remains inflected with ethnocentric dimensions and is limited by the analysis of culture within homogeneous national units (p8).

In mapping the complex terrain of contemporary British Asian dance music, *Dis-Orienting Rhythms* takes on a series of problematics which, the editors claim, have tended to characterise the critique of its genres within the discourses of cultural studies. According to Sharma et al., their 'risky project ... exposes the Eurocentric limits of the celebration of hybrid Otherness' (p1). Within this agenda, the emphasis is on dis-orientalising the discourses on Asian musics, simultaneously highlighting the problematics of orientating oneself within their geographic, national, and ethnic boundaries, while acknowledging the properly disorientating nature of such a generically profligate field. Against the simplistic idea that 'ethnically' hybrid forms are inherently and unproblematically postmodern or politically radical, *Dis-Orienting Rhythms* aims to lance the boil of 'liberal multiculturalism' (p3) and to open a space in which the Asian practitioners, consumers and critics of these musics are given their own voice, rather than being the object of the sometimes unconsciously ethnocentric discourses of British academia. In this, the 'risky project' nevertheless claims to work towards 'a pedagogy committed to the construction of forms of political engagement that do not reduce popular culture to the scrutinized Other' (p3). And in attempting to speak from 'within' the culture of Asian dance musics, the project becomes an exploration of 'how these musics may be identified or (re)claimed as being "Asian" in Britain' (p8).

Ashwani Sharma's paper, 'Sounds Oriental: The (Im)possibility of Theorizing Asian Musical Cultures', begins from the idea that '[t]he corrosive hybridity of post-colonial Asian dance music ruptures the ordered silence of contemporary Britain' (p15). This at once risks a position which the book as a whole claims to disavow, but also apparently flattens out the field of musical culture with Asian Britain into a mute homogeneous anonymity barely recognisable in actuality. No doubt this passage has a certain provocative power, yet while Sharma succeeds in qualifying his concept of hybridity and extending it beyond simplistic assumptions as to its radicality (as well as engagingly traversing the problematics of authenticity within his chosen hybrid), he nevertheless fails to qualify his claim of

Britain's 'ordered silence' in the multiple spaces beyond the confines of Asian musics.

Sanjay Sharma's 'Noisy Asians or "Asian Noise"' deals with the thorny issue of how one remains a politically, culturally envoiced subject under the sign of postmodernity. On the one hand, there has been the traditional tendency to read identity through the lens of essentialist historiography, while on the other is the postmodern tendency to de-essentialise the subject, simultaneously risking the dissolution of crucial aspects of identity and the political vocality which is attendant upon it. For Sharma, essentialism and its concepts are intimately tied into colonialist attitudes: for example, certain 'white' writers tracing the shift from Bhangra to post-Bhangra have often discursively risked 'an authenticity problematic that sustains a neo-Orientalist understanding of anterior Asian youth cultural formations' (p36) due to their over-emphasis of the primacy of Bhangra's Punjabi 'roots'. For Sharma, however, the contemporary reality lies within the plural, rather than an originary singularity, yet without necessitating a theoretical investment in 'the relativist pluralism of a status quo multiculturalist politics' (p55). Rather, Sharma recommends that we shift into a 'third space' (p55) between identity politics and its supposed postmodern erasure, a space of discursive 'risk and possibility' (p55).

In 'Repetitive Beatings or Criminal Justice?', John Hutnyk traces through the politics of that most notorious of anti-dance music shibboleths, the 1994 Criminal Justice Act, with its infamous clause regarding 'sounds wholly or predominantly characterized by the emission of a succession of repetitive beats.' However, Hutnyk's main emphasis here is on the parliamentary debates surrounding the Act, specifically as they related to issues of racist attacks and the control of youth culture. In an often amusing, if slightly journalistic, style, he recounts a number of highlights from his own experience of the debates as a visitor to the House, homing in on a number of essentialist assumptions which various MPs based their speeches on. Overall, Hutnyk continues the assault on 'racist, essentialist, head-in-sand nostalgias for authenticity', but claims that '[b]ands like FunDaMental blow this kind of neo-Orientalism out of the water' (p161). The basis for this claim derives from his reading of the video for their song 'Dog-Tribe', 'banned' by TV stations for its allegedly Islamic fundamentalist response to racist attacks against Asian youth. For Hutnyk, the 'banning' of FunDaMental's video becomes symptomatic of the ways in which political and media discourses operate in the vague space of double standards. Moreover, he attacks academic complacency and silence on these issues, accusing 'comfortable intellectuals' (p186) of a tacit acceptance of the political status quo under the Tory government: '[t]he task is to wake up from this stupor – this book is not simply an essay in cultural studies' (p161).

More canonically academic in tone and purpose is the final paper by Raminder Kaur and Virinder Kalra, 'New Paths for South Asian Identity and Musical Creativity', which aims to lay out 'a theoretical tract for localized and transnational forms of identity' (p218) in order to analyse Bhangra enthnographically. In so doing, they coin a number of new terms, such as 'Br-Asian', replacing what they call '[t]he over-used and poorly defined category "British Asian"... problematic as it essentializes both terms, as well as hierarchizing the former against the latter' (p219). Evidently, 'Br-Asian' truncates the hierarchical term while leaving the specificity of the heading 'Asian' intact. Yet while the potential essentialism of a term evidently does lie in its definition, surely this is grounded more in its usage, which is inherently multiple in itself? Equally, 'Br-Asian' still seems rather loose (or essentialising – take your pick) in its retention of the second term in full. Subsequent to this, however, Kaur and Kalra shift their focus onto their 'deconstructive term', 'Transl-Asia', reflective of the multiplicity contained within the concept of the Asian, as well as the diasporic, cross-national multiplicity which marks the 'Asian' experience documented within the book as a whole. Citing these two new theoretical terms in the final paragraph of the book, Kaur and Kalra claim that such terms 'enable us to slash out new paths, new routes by which to challenge media and other ideological formations and their reliance upon unproblematized "ethnic" categories' (p230).

Overall, the papers discussed above (and those not discussed) attempt to carve out a theoretical territory marked by a feeling of radical newness. However, while the authors tend to approach all standard critical theories from a sober and considered critical distance, never fully coming down in favour of one or the other modish orthodoxy, very little in the way of new theory *qua* new theory has been achieved here. The main strength lies in their engagement with a field of musical genres marginalised within the mainstreams of academic discourse; in this, it is one of the first important collections of essays on Asian musics within 'Britain'. Yet here we come up against an interesting site of ethnic contestation once again. This is, in fact, not really a book about Asians in Britain. Its concentration on England and its assumption of a hegemonic 'white' culture in Britain betrays a certain anglocentrism lurking beneath its quest for the problematisation of Br-Asian culture. Little is made of the question of what Britain itself today is: a question of particular importance to, amongst others, Asians in Scotland or Wales who have two basic reasons for mistrusting the 'white' centre of Britain, and at a time when the whole constitutional and cultural fabric of the so-called 'United' Kingdom is being debated (often with the terms of post-colonial theory). This is a debate which has an impact upon all cultural groups within the UK, and which might suggest a shift in discourses on Britain away from an exclusively anglocentric perspective. In writing so blithely of 'the invisibility of whiteness', it would perhaps be wise – particularly today – to avoid assuming an invisibility of Englishness. Britain, particularly in the 1990s, no longer speaks with an English voice.

Nevertheless, this passionately written and ground-breaking text is a timely addition to the growing corpus of post-colonial writings on music. Musicology is often a late-starter in coming to terms with critical theories prevalent within other humanities disciplines, and post-colonial theory is merely the latest in a series of musicological late starts. The fact that this book is written from within the discipline of cultural studies rather than from within musicology itself merely confirms once more the pattern of influence which has tended to mark the rise of popular musicology. It is all too easy for the musicologist to dismiss a book such as this in terms of its failure to engage analytically with the formalist shibboleth of 'TMI' ('The Music Itself'), as if sociological, ideological, political and overall cultural contexts were not intimately bound up with the production and consumption of music. However, it is perhaps time for musicologists *qua* musicologists to wake up and take notice of the genres discussed within *Dis-Orienting Rhythms*. Hopefully, this book will serve as a text of disorientation to provoke just such a response, and many others.

The Centre for New Ethnicities Research

The Centre for New Ethnicities Research brings together staff at the University of East London concerned about issues of race and ethnicity, to work on research, education and other common projects. Based in the Department of Cultural Studies, the Centre has since 1991 developed innovative thinking and practice in its field. The centre was established partly as a response to the emergence of a cultural politics in which hybridity and diaspora, rather than roots and race, had become central themes.

The Centre has developed links with many leading academics in Europe, Africa, the Americas and the Indian subcontinent through its external research associate network and visiting professor programme. Our international reputation as a centre of intellectual excellence has been recognised by the award of the top five star rating by the Higher Education Funding Council in the recent Research Assessment Exercise.

The Centre's perspective is interdisciplinary, drawing on cultural studies, sociology, political science, psychology, history and the arts. The focus of much of our work is on exploring the links between local cultures and communities of East London and global patterns of immigration, settlement, and national identity.

From the outset the Centre has tried to link its academic research to practical interventions in the field of ant-racist work and inter-cultural education with young people living in areas of high racial tension.

Community Art is an important thread running through much of the Centre's educational work with young people. The Youth Arts Project was an important component of the *Frontlines BackYards* conference and led to a separate exhibition under the title *Making a Difference - Youth Arts in East London* in July 1997. A report of the exhibition has been published, featuring colour illustrations of the work of 87 students from the four schools in the London Borough of Newham that formed the exhibition. Background material on the project including an essay by the curator is also included.

Many of our curriculum packs produced for use in schools and INSET are based on media and cultural studies work with young people. The *Tricks of the Trade* Project has involved educationalists, researchers and artists in producing a set of multi-media teaching materials around themes drawn from the African Diaspora. Other materials include *Playgrounds of Prejudice* which explores questions of bullying and racist name calling; the *Seeing Through Racism Exhibition,* and a new pack *Wish You Weren't Here,* which looks at issues of race and representation through Edwardian Postcards.

The Centre's public seminar, lecture and conference programme is a crucial part of our dissemination strategy. Our conference on the theme of *FrontLines BackYards,* detailed in this journal, drew a large international audience of delegates and participants together in two days of debates, presentations and performances around issues of black cultural politics and the changing geographies of race, nation and ethnicity in the post modern world.

Recent seminar series have been on *Issues in Refugee Studies, New Directions in Psychoanalysis and Racism* and *Rethinking Eurocentrism.* In spring 1998 a series is being held at the Institute of Education entitled *Race, Education and the Multicultural Society.*

Every year the Centre invites a distinguished speaker who has made a major contribution to thinking or policy making to deliver a special guest lecture. Stuart Hall gave the first, Zygmunt Bauman the second, followed by Bhiku Parekh on *Rethinking Multiculturalism,* Etienne Balibar on *Racism in Europe* and Patricia Hill Collins on *African American Women and the Politics of Containment.* These lectures are all available on video.

This year Professor E.A. 'Archie' Markham will be giving a Reading / Lecture at the University of East London on 13 May entitled *The Language of a Country.*

In the last two years the unit has developed its own publications list. In addition to the exhibition report detailed above we have a varied list including learned monographs on 'post colonial theory'; research reports; working papers based on staff research; and an innovative series of staff training videos for use in equal opportunities work. Our regular Newsletter *New Ethnicities* details the ongoing work of the centre. A book of collected essays by members of the Centre, entitled *New Ethnicities, New Racisms* is due to be published by Zed Books in 1998.

For further information please contact:
Richard McKeever, Centre for New Ethnicities Research,
University of East London, Longbridge Road,
Dagenham, RM8 2AS
Tel 0181 590 7000 (ext.2632)
Fax 0181 849 3598
e-mail r.mckeever@uel.ac.uk

Frontlines Backyards: The Video

Frontlines Backyards: The Video is not so much a documentary record of the conference as an exploration of the cultural politics of the event itself.

Drawing on **original interviews** with the organisers, plenary speakers and workshop contributors, as well as off-the-cuff responses from those attending, the programme looks at some of the **key points of engagement** within the changing agenda of race in Britain.

Statements in **music, drama, performance poetry and photography** are woven into the debates, while the contribution of the rising generation is highlighted with material from a youth arts programme in which more than two hundred school students participated.

Especially recommended for use in A level and undergraduate teaching and for youth/community groups.

This twenty minute VHS video is available for **£15.00** from the **Centre for New Ethnicities Research, University of East London, Longbridge Road, Dagenham RM8 2AS**

Telephone enquiries: 0181 590 7000 x2632

Making a Difference to Youth Arts in London

A report of the successful Youth Arts exhibition *Making a Difference* has been published by the Centre for New Ethnicities Research at the University of East London.

The Youth Arts Exhibition grew from *Frontlines Backyards* Conference. This innovative project developed new ideas for visual arts education.

The report features colour illustrations of the work of 87 students from four schools in the London Borough of Newham, which formed the *Making a Difference* exhibition. Background material on the project is included as well as an essay by the curator.

Making a Difference: Youth Arts in East London is available from the **Centre for New Ethnicities Research, University of East London, Longbridge Road, Dagenham RM8 2AS** priced **£8.00**

Telephone enquiries: 0181-590 7000 x2632

MA and Postgraduate Diploma in Refugee Studies

One year full-time
Two years part-time

•Introduction to forced migration. •Migration, citizenship and social policy.
•International refugee law. •Cultures of exile.
•Research Methods. •Independent dissertation.

The programme will interest those concerned with migration, ethnicity and diasporic studies; social, legal and cultural theory; human rights and refugee advocacy.

Further information from
Refugee Studies, Dept of Cultural Studies
University of East London, Longbridge Road.
Dagenham, Essex RM8 2AS
Tel 0181 590 7000 ext.2741
e-mail Wells3@uel.ac.uk

FACULTY OF SOCIAL SCIENCES

UNIVERSITY *of*
EAST LONDON

Parallax

a journal of metadiscursive theory and cultural practices

Editors

Joanne Morra and **Marquard Smith**
*Centre for Cultural Studies, Department of Fine Art, University of Leeds, Leeds, LS2 9JT, UK
Email: parallax@leeds.ac.uk*

Scope

Parallax is an exciting and provocative cultural studies journal which seeks to initiate alternative forms of cultural theory and criticism through a critical engagement with the production of cultural knowledges.

Parallax will be of interest to those working in many areas including critical theory, cultural history, gender studies, philosophy, queer theory, english and comparative literature, post-colonial theory, art history and of course, cultural studies.

Recent issues include

- cultural studies and philosophy
- theory and practice
- dissonant feminisms
- kojève's paris.now bataille

Subscription Information

Vol. 4 (1998), Quarterly
ISSN 1353-4645
Institutional: US$198/£120
Personal: US$58/£35

Visit the Journal's Web Site
http://www.tandf.co.uk/

Now Published by Taylor & Francis

Free Email Contents Service

To sign up for our free contents service for this title, send an email to:
mailserv@tandf.co.uk
with *lists* in the body of the message to receive further instructions

Visit the T&F Web Site

http://www.tandf.co.uk/
or
http://tandfdc.com/

The Publishers

Taylor & Francis Publishers
1 Gunpowder Square
London, EC4A 3DE, UK
Tel: +44 (0) 171 583 0490
Fax: + 44 (0) 171 583 0585
or
1900 Frost Road, Suite 101
Bristol, PA 19007-1598, USA
Tel: +1 800 821 8312
+1 215 785 5800
Fax: +1 215 785 5515

Email: info@tandf.co.uk
info@tandfpa.com

Free Sample Copies Available

JPLXAA4-0997

Critical Quarterly

BLACKWELL Journals

Edited by Colin MacCabe

Critical Quarterly has been at the forefront of literary criticism since the 1960's and has established an international reputation for its unique blend of fiction, criticism and poetry which mix together to reflect contemporary issues.

Centre for Psychoanalytic Studies

University of Essex, Colchester CO4 3SQ
        (45 mins by Intercity from London)
1998-1999 innovative MA & PhD schemes:
* Psychoanalytic Studies
* Gender & Generativity in Psychoanalysis
* The Psychoanalysis of Groups & Organizations
* Reproduction & Perinatal Psychodynamics
* Psychoanalysis, Psychosis & Health Care
* Psychoanalysis & Philosophy
* Jungian & Post-Jungian Studies
Also available: a variety of accredited short courses
Details: **tel**:01206 873745   **fax:** 01206 872746
e-mail:marilynw@essex.ac.uk or **postal address** above

Body & Society

Edited by **Mike Featherstone** *Nottingham Trent University* and **Bryan S Turner** *Deakin University*

'Body & Society gives critical work on the body from a multitude of disciplines a regular appearance in print. Reading each article alone would be enlightening; I have found reading them together to be exhilarating.' - **Emily Martin**

Highlights from Volume 3 (1997) Include:

▶ **Harvey Ferguson** on the accumulation of body-images in Western Society

▶ **Anoop Nayak** on disclosing whiteness in Haagen-Dazs advertising

▶ **Claire Colebrook** on feminism and autonomy

▶ **Tia DeNora** on music and erotic agency

▶ **Deborah Lupton and Greg Noble** on dehumanizing strategies in personal computer use

▶ **Nick Crossley** on corporeality and communicative action

▶ **Alex Hughes and Anne Witz** on feminism and the matter of bodies

Published quarterly • ISSN: 1357-034X

For details about special rates for TCS subscribers and the availability of back issues of the journal contact the Journals Marketing Department at the address below.

Visit the SAGE website: http://www.sagepub.co.uk/

BACK ISSUES

Why not Subscribe?

New Formations is published three times a year. Make sure of your copy by subscribing.

SUBSCRIPTION RATES FOR 1997/98 (3 ISSUES)

Individual Subscriptions
UK   £35.00
Rest of World   £38.00

Institutional Subscriptions
UK   £70.00
Rest of World   £75.00

Please send one year's subscription
starting with Issue Number ————————————————

I enclose payment of ————————————————————

Please send me ———— copies of back issue no. ——————

I enclose total payment of ——————————————————

Name ——————————————————————————————

Address ————————————————————————————————

———————————————————————— Postcode ——————————

Please return this form with cheque or money order (sterling only) payable to *Lawrence & Wishart* and send to:
Lawrence and Wishart, 99a Wallis Road, London E9 5LN